Trouble Spots in Taxation

TAFT MEMORIAL FUND LECTURES

1946

UNIVERSITY OF CINCINNATI

The first of a projected series of volumes of University of Cincinnati Public Lectures, the delivery and publication of which is made possible by the Charles Phelps Taft Memorial Fund of the University of Cincinnati.

Trouble Spots in Taxation

Essays in the Philosophy of Taxation and Other Public Finance Problems

By HAROLD M. GROVES

PRINCETON
PRINCETON UNIVERSITY PRESS
FOR THE UNIVERSITY OF CINCINNATI
1948

336.2
G919t

CONTENTS

Trouble Spots in Taxation

CHAPTER I
Taxation and Equality

Introduction

THIS series of essays will explore some of the philosophical roots and branches of public finance. We begin where analyses of taxation usually begin—that is, with a search for some principle, or rule, or scale of values that will serve as a touchstone to judge proposed patterns for the distribution of taxes. We shall find that an individual's philosophy of equality and inequality must play an important role in this analysis. However, at the outset, some observations concerning conflict in taxation seem necessary.

Conflict in Taxation

If it is conflict that makes life interesting, taxation should be one of the world's most fascinating subjects. Our theme is a field of battle, both for opposing interests and opposing viewpoints. As to the former, there are those who see in taxation nothing but a power contest between organized interest groups. But this interpretation, although containing a large element of truth, is both too sweeping and too simple. It is too sweeping because taxation is not all conflict; there are important elements of harmony in the picture. There are areas in taxation where reasonable men might get together even though their sympathies were at opposite poles. Jones might favor high surtaxes and Smith oppose them; yet both could perhaps agree that a carry-over of business losses would be fair and desirable. Then too, most reasonable men might get together on a few general goals, such as the preservation of a democratic way of life and a rising national income. It is highly important to seek areas of agreement because conflict can become so predominant as to make living together impossible. Common goals might include the prevention of this catastrophe.

[3]

Conflict is not a *simple* tug-of-war between opposing interests because one may find his loyalty divided among several. For instance, territorial interests may compete with class or industrial interests. A senator from a mining state may favor farmers as against mine companies but he may also fight for his mining constituents against rival interests located in other states. Then too, there is the old distinction between short-run and long-run interests. Self-aggrandizement at the expense of others may look attractive in the short view but disastrous as long-range policy. The self-interest of a particular business may conflict with good policy for business as a whole. These distinctions are what critics have in mind when they conclude that the businessman is often his own worst enemy.

As to conflicting viewpoints among public-finance scholars, one must begin by conceding that most of the field is controversial. There is very little in taxation to hand out as "accepted doctrine." Critics differ in their preference for one tax or another because they have different values, different philosophies of life, different kinds of worlds in which they would choose to live. Of course, there are aspects of taxation, such as shifting and incidence, that involve problems entirely divorced from tastes and preferences. Unfortunately, scholars do not agree too well even on these matters. The difficulty is not one of subjective differences; it is due to the complexity of the phenomena examined, to the many variables involved, and to the impossibility of exposing hypotheses to controlled experiment or other precise verification.

Thus a public-finance writer finds himself in the unenviable position where most of what he might say could be contradicted by someone at least as competent and well informed as himself. To a large extent this is true of economics and economists generally. It has been said that economists stretched end to and across the country would fail to reach—an agreement! To some this is "Exhibit A" of the "lamentable state

[4]

of economics." To others, it is an indication that economists dabble too much in areas where they find it impossible to be "scientific." The author shares neither of these reactions. Of course, it is desirable where possible to enlarge the area within our field where truth has been demonstrated with scientific precision. However, it does not follow that economists should avoid the remainder of the field nor that they should be reproached for disagreement. The layman must pass judgment on controversial issues and he is entitled to aid from the economist. The latter can help the layman analyze his problem clearly and intelligently although each may draw an independent conclusion. The economist can lead the way to a scientific attitude, even if he does not always arrive at an authoritative conclusion, not by avoiding conclusions, but by giving both sides a hearing, by labeling the controversial as such, and by introspection and candor concerning biases. The author has scant sympathy for the view that economists should deal only with means and remain neutral as to ends.[1] This inhibition could "cramp his style" considerably in these essays should he allow himself to be thus "fenced in." After this declaration of independence, it is comforting to reflect that even physicists are now concerned about the ends to be served by some of their recent handiwork.

Principles of Tax Distribution

Most of us belong to some organization—such as a club or a church—that has a treasurer, ways and means of raising money, a surplus or a deficit, and a "financial problem." There are many such organizations but the grandest of all is the government, differing from the others in that membership and contributions to the treasury are compulsory. The problem before us concerns the plans for distributing, or determining, the dues that you and I should pay to this most eminent of clubs.

[1] *See* Lionel Robbins, *An Essay on the Nature and Significance of Economic Science*, 2nd ed., Macmillan, London, 1935.

PER CAPITA DISTRIBUTION

Of course, the simplest way to distribute the tax load would be a universal poll or per capita tax at an equal amount per head. This pattern of distribution finds ample precedent in the private sphere. Most clubs charge their members a flat fee. The bill for government at present writing would amount to some $40 for each of us. (The author personally would be very happy to settle his account with all governments at $240 for his family of six!) This system of distribution would achieve a certain specious neutrality. However, the community would rightly regard it as intolerable. We would start at once to advocate "exceptions." Some would want to exempt babies, and others would seek a favorable classification for students, lunatics, veterans, and perhaps even women. We would thus demonstrate that we consider it as bad to treat unequals equally as to treat equals unequally.

BENEFITS RECEIVED

Another doctrine holds that all taxes should be based on the principle of benefits received. The taxpayer should buy government as he buys gas from the gas company—so much used, so much paid for. This theory is used plausibly to justify the state motor fuel taxes. The more we drive on the public highways, the more fuel we use; the more fuel we use, the more taxes we pay to the state. Thus the motor fuel tax is a sort of fee for highway use.

It would not be so simple, however, to apply the same principle to payment for *all* governmental services. No meter yet devised is capable of measuring the cost or value of the multitudinous services each of us gets from government. For instance, how would the value of a new battleship be divided among the people of the United States—people with varying wealth and income, some on the seaboard, others in the interior; some engaged in foreign trade, others not; and so forth? Would the fact that some regard the navy as ample without this new ship have any relevance?

The truth is of course that we enjoy these services collectively in our corporate capacity as *the public*, and any division is sure to seem artificial and forced—a rationalization supporting a preexisting conclusion. Benefits received often make any tax plausible but they afford little basis for a choice among taxes. Thus the fact that local governments render essential services supports equally well a poll tax, property tax, or business tax. What would happen to any of these bases if the government were abstracted from the picture?

Then too, public opinion supports the wide use of many public services that would be impossible were the direct beneficiaries to pay for what they receive. We have compulsory-school-attendance laws requiring all children below a certain age to attend school whether or not they wish and whether or not their parents can afford to send them. Since probably less than a third of our people receive systematic dental care, many feel that it would be in the public interest to provide this care at taxpayers' expense. They are seeking to circumvent the limitations on consumption which the benefit principle imposes.

ABILITY TO PAY

Another principle upon which taxes might be distributed is that of ability to pay. This is the principle upon which, in the private sphere, churches and many other "philanthropies" are financed. The church finance committee expects parishioners to "help out" on the church budget according to their means. Why not do the same with government? One difficulty here is that ability to pay is likely to mean "all things to all men." The phrase is likely to appear in all party platforms and this alone makes its clarity suspect. Ability to pay can be used to support a tax proportionate to income; that is, twice as much income, twice as much tax. It can also be used to support a graduated (progressive) tax; for example, twice as much income, four times as much tax. And it may be used to support a levy that confiscates most or all of the higher incomes, leveling distribution as it goes, down to the point where governmental needs are satisfied. Ability-to-pay doctrine can give no precise answer to the question: Is an 85 percent top income tax rate justified?

The ability-to-pay concepts are based in part upon the marginal-utility theory of income. According to this view, as income advances, the importance of another dollar more or less decreases. Thus, taxing the higher incomes involves a lesser sacrifice than obtaining revenue at the bottom of the income scale.

Sacrifice theories of taxation have been subject to many criticisms. One is that the value of money and the pain of taxes to individuals is a psychological phenomenon, impossible to measure, and differing among individuals according to temperament. Additional income may mean much to "A," who is materialistic, and very little to "B," whose interest in life runs in other directions. "A" may need funds for capital in his business; "B" may be amply supplied. Sir Josiah Stamp described the problem of measuring sacrifice as follows: "It is very difficult for a man to say quantitatively that one boot pinches *three* times as much as the other, even where both are his own, and how much more difficult is it for one man to say that his boot pinches twice as much as another's!"[2]

The marginal-utility theory seems most realistic when applied to consumption; its validity is doubtful for the dollars that satisfy only acquisitive interests. In the latter case it

[2] Sir Josiah Stamp, *The Fundamental Principles of Taxation*, Macmillan, London, 1923, pp. 53-54.

may often be true that the more one gets, the more one wants (and perhaps needs).[3]

These objections to the sacrifice theory have been answered as follows: Individual differences must be disregarded in favor of a general rule, which should conform to the public's judgment that for the *average* person the importance of income does diminish as more is acquired. If precise measurement is impossible, common sense will suffice as authority for the differentiation and its degree. Moreover, sacrifice has objective as well as subjective aspects. Society may consider it more important that "A" can supply himself with a newspaper and dental care than that "B" have a second automobile. This preference may be quite independent of the interests and appetites of the two individuals. The latter approach seems to throw sacrifice and marginal utility overboard; but it can be argued that it only substitutes social comparisons for individual ones.

The ability-to-pay doctrine rests in part on "faculty" as distinguished from "sacrifice" considerations. The faculty approach emphasizes differences among individuals in their *capacities* to support government. The differences may be due to variation in talents or to other circumstances. The claim for service according to capacity is strongest in time of emergency. With the appearance of a war or a flood, a community develops solidarity rapidly, regards itself as a family, and expects services from its members according to their economic and perhaps even their physical strength. Those who have youth and vigor are expected to defend the community even at the risk of their lives. Less may be demanded of others because they have less to give, but each is expected to do his part.

Of course, the private sphere in which both sacrifice and faculty considerations are given greatest scope is the family.

[3] M. Slade Kendrick, "Ability-to-Pay Theory of Taxation," *American Economic Review*, xxix (Mar. 1939), 92-101.

And even it shows more solidarity at some times than others: witness its chastened attitudes when there is serious illness or a funeral. Psychologists and biologists would probably agree that man's unselfishness and sense of brotherhood, exalted by all religions, originated in the animal world from the instinct of parents, particularly mothers, to care for their young. "It is not the habit of mothers to lavish care on the strong and forget the delicate." Idealists see a wider and wider application of this concern culminating in the universal view that all men are brothers.

Some students have found the sacrifice and faculty approach to tax distribution so unsatisfactory that they have cast it aside entirely. They have justified heavier taxes on the rich than on the poor (if at all) solely in terms of the conviction that inequalities are excessive and that taxation is a convenient means of reducing them. Interest in equality certainly has a bearing on tax judgments (about which, more later) but this sweeping renunciation of ability to pay goes too far. A doctrine having so many applications in the private sphere—applications quite independent of any concern about distribution—can be the valid basis of a preference among tax patterns for government. Of course, there is no "scientific" obligation to take this somewhat philanthropic view of government and of taxpayers' duty. One can insist on the right to believe that government should function more like a business organization. Nevertheless, it can be said that ability to pay is a valid basis for *one* tax philosophy. It will give no precise quantitative answers, but neither will any other doctrine.

EQUALITY OF OPPORTUNITY

As previously suggested, the question of tax distribution may be approached exclusively from the standpoint of concern about inequalities. Obviously, this aspect of the problem merits more than passing consideration. Here, we must start by distinguishing two kinds of equality. The first, *equality of opportunity*, propounds that we should all start at the same tapeline and go as fast and as far as our natural endowments will carry us. This gives all an equal chance but does not interfere with results otherwise. Unfair competition and special privilege are condemned. Put another way, the idea is to allow full reward for economic achievement resulting from subjective differences, but to render the objective environment neutral to all comers.

Our Puritan forebears subscribed to the philosophy that "fools should be allowed and required to act freely and then be held for the consequences of their folly."[4] The weak and irresponsible were entitled to a fair chance in life, but beyond this they had no claim upon those who were better endowed or who made better use of their endowments. Similarly, the strong and provident owed nothing to those less able "to get on in life." This is known as the "individualistic philosophy" and it is quite in accord with the equality-of-opportunity theory.

This equality doctrine looks conservative, and it does have a conservative following. But it also has very radical implications. The institution of inheritance, since the days of John Stuart Mill, at least, has been challenged on the ground of special privilege. Inheritance gives some youth a long head-start in life, leaving others to catch up if they can. On the other hand, abolition of inheritance, while it might reduce inequalities of opportunity (as might other measures) could never eliminate them entirely. Children reared in rich families would have an economic advantage even though they were forced "to swim for themselves" after the death of their parents. Thus, full equality of opportunity is unattainable without a general equality of income.

4 Roscoe Pound, *The Spirit of the Common Law*, quoted in Ralph Barton Perry, *Puritanism and Democracy*, Vanguard Press, New York, 1944, p. 288.

EQUALITY OF INCOME

This leads to a discussion of the second kind of economic equality—*equality of rewards* or *equality of income*. Professor Graham expresses the opinion that equality of opportunity should be the ideal of equalitarians, that going beyond this would be to "deliver the world to parasites who would quickly drain it of its blood,"[5] and that only the sub-average "would want a dead equality of income."[6] But he must be wrong in the latter conclusion. George Bernard Shaw, at least, is opposed to all economic inequality;[7] and whatever may be his other limitations, no one would accuse him of being sub-average. The equalitarian unlimited regards a desire for inequality as bad taste—like the conduct of a guest who might help himself to all or nearly all of his host's meat and potatoes. Many others, who do not go so far, object to the prevailing degree of inequality. Barbara Wootton, in her *Lament for Economics*, states this position as follows:

"When I review the evidence of undernourishment, miserable housing and lack of amenities of civilized living generally, along side of sybaritic luxury, which obtrude themselves upon the notice of any casual observer in any great city of most of Europe and America, I find it difficult to convince myself that we really could not, if we cared to try, distribute our resources in a way which would give greater aggregate satisfaction than this."[8]

Democracy is a broad term with many meanings. Some usage, at least, supports a definition wide enough to include a measure of economic equality. One suspects that this is what the Russians are talking about when they claim that their

[5] Frank D. Graham, *Social Goals and Economic Institutions*, Princeton University Press, 1942, p. 17.
[6] *Ibid.*
[7] See, for instance, George Bernard Shaw, *The Intelligent Woman's Guide to Socialism and Capitalism*, Brentano's, New York, 1928.
[8] Barbara Wootton, *Lament for Economics*, George Allen & Unwin, London, 1938, pp. 210-11.

country is more democratic than the United States. Beyond this, many political philosophers have long contended that the existence of extreme inequalities is a threat to democratic institutions. For instance, equal participation in government (voting) may lose significance if a few people of great wealth obtain control of most newspapers.

Possible Rules for Income Distribution

In economic literature several rules for the ideal distribution of income have been suggested. One is: "To each according to his works." This sounds like the familiar and conservative slogan: "Every man is entitled to the fruits of his own labor." Both leave unsettled the vitally important question of whether one is entitled to use the fruits of his labor to produce more fruits, that is, whether private property in productive goods is to be permitted. Reward according to product is the principle applied in present-day Russia and, as there interpreted, individuals are mainly excluded from the ownership of productive property. Notwithstanding this limitation, several reports on Russia have observed that inequalities of income there are little, if any, less than in the United States.

Another formula is: "From each according to his ability; to each according to his needs." This is the slogan that Karl Marx thought too extreme for full application until men and institutions had been conditioned under a less extensive socialism.

Still another principle is: "Subsistence to all before abundance to a few." This type of slogan supports social security and other programs aiming at a minimum of income or of governmental services.

Finally, there is the more pragmatic "common-sense" type of slogan: "Reduce inequalities to the degree that is practical without destroying necessary incentives for economic progress."

[13]

Equality Through Public Expenditure on Social Services

Of course, the interest in equality is served quite as well by public expenditure on the social services as by taxation.[9] Indeed, a principal proponent of equality, R. H. Tawney, places greatest faith in the development of the social services, observing: "What is important is not that all men should receive the same pecuniary income. It is that the surplus resources of society should be so husbanded and applied that it is a matter of minor significance whether they receive it or not."[10] If education, housing, medical care, and nutrition were provided at common expense, or adequate standards in these areas were underwritten by the taxpayer as a "national minimum," the dignity of the individual and his cultural opportunities would be assured. Under these circumstances, inequalities would lose much of their present importance. Socialization of consumption has received less attention than socialization of production, but its potentialities are hardly less radical.

How Much Inequality Do We Want?

How much inequality and personal competition do we want? Perhaps the question can be brought home to college students by asking them: How would you like a system of grading under which the student would compete with himself rather than his fellow-students? It could be worked something like this: Every student would be given a capacity rating at the beginning of his college career. It could be based on his intelligence rating and his background experience. His class grades would then depend upon how his work measured up to his rating. Thus, if he surpassed expectations he would

---

[9] However, public expenditures necessitate taxation and the effect of the latter may be amplified or counteracted by the pattern chosen for the former. Thus even a proportional tax combined with a high expenditure for social services might involve substantial equalization.

[10] R. H. Tawney, *Equality*, George Allen & Unwin, London, 1931, p. 155.

get an "A"; if he fell below them he might get a "C" or a "D" or even worse. I think there is much to be said for such an innovation but I would not expect the majority of students or faculty members to pass favorably upon it.

Inequality and Economic Progress

Of course, the "million-dollar question" is: To what extent, if at all, does the reduction of inequalities interfere with economic progress and full employment? Professor Harley Lutz would have us believe that the problem of serious unemployment and the income tax both started in this country in 1913 and that this was no odd coincidence. His simple recipe for prosperity is: "If you want to make a dollar by any honest means you are free to try, and if you succeed you may keep it."[11] Or again: "Concretely and in terms of an historical parallel, it is the choice between the Ford fortune and the Ford automobile. If ... [we] should decide that there shall be no more fortunes, ... [we shall] also thereby decide that there shall be no commodities of mass comfort and enjoyment other than those now known."[12]

Recently the author heard a report from a traveler returned from Poland. The food shortage there, he said, was due in part to the fact that people had failed to plant gardens. This in turn was due to the fact that the chances of harvesting were seriously reduced by marauders. Only a few found the prospect of relieving the hunger of others an adequate incentive.

It is clear enough that in a world short of Utopia *some* inequalities are necessary. But what about the degree? Is it true that we must forego reducing inequalities on pain of halting or reversing economic progress? The following considerations should be weighed in searching for an answer.

11 Harley L. Lutz, *Guideposts to a Free Economy*, McGraw-Hill, New York, 1945, p. 206.
12 *Ibid.*, p. 82.

1. It is urged by a large school of economists—the Keynesians—that reducing inequalities is positively favorable (not to say necessary) to the growth of the national income. This view is sometimes described as "purchasing power economics." It holds that in the present state of our technological development, the limiting factor is the availability of adequate markets. We could and would produce more if we knew how to dispose of it. This doctrine is often invoked by labor leaders in support of higher wage demands. However, even before the war, Ralph Flanders, a businessman, sized up our industrial potential as follows: "All engineers know that if an engineer-dictator over industry could be appointed and given complete control over raw materials, machinery and trained labor, we could flood, bury and smother the people under an avalanche of goods and services such as no Utopian dreamer in his busiest slumbers ever imagined."[13]

At a time when one must order a new automobile a year in advance, it may seem unduly optimistic (or perhaps pessimistic) to worry about inadequate markets. Our economic system received during the war, in the form of expanded bank credit, a shot in the arm the like of which we had never before witnessed in this country. But what will the situation be after the shot wears off? It seems more than likely that markets will prove of much greater concern than shortage of goods.

However, it is said that markets can be created equally well either by wide consumption or high investment. Taxes which promote the former may discourage the latter. Taxes on higher incomes may not reduce saving and encourage consumption so much as they reduce venture capital, diverting it into secure investments. Thus we cannot be sure, at least, that reducing inequalities favors economic progress. On the other hand, investment itself cannot be justified in the long run except by prospects of consumption.

[13] Quoted from Stuart Chase, *The Economy of Abundance*, Macmillan, New York, 1934, p. 14.

2. There are taxes and taxes, just as there is "more than one way to skin a rabbit." The death tax may have one effect on incentives and the income tax another, although the two are comparable as equalizers.

3. Wealth and income do not result alone from industry and thrift. It is equally possible to become wealthy by obstructing or by promoting production. Wealth is acquired from findings and stealings as well as from earnings. To tax away these impurities in the flow of income would be ideal; as a practical matter, qualitative differentiation is difficult.[14] However, the existence of large elements of "unearned" income affords some justification for quantitative taxation, which might otherwise be rejected on the score that the fruits of one's labor must be allowed as an incentive.

Big incomes may be viewed as giving recipients an extravagant living standard; or as serving their acquisitive appetites; or as providing them with an instrument to manage "in trust." It is in his role as trustee that the big-income recipient is most persuasive. This is especially true when he has been chosen for his function not by inheritance but by competition. But the genius of trustees may be devoted solely to serving their own interests with little or no regard for the supposed beneficiary of the trust (society). The old notion that one cannot "give himself a lift" without also serving the social good has been punctured so often and so completely that further punishment here would be superfluous. Moreover, it is not established that trustees can give society the benefit of their genius only by *owning* large amounts of capital in their own right; they can also assemble and manage the capital of others.

4. The "fruits of one's labor" are fairly obvious in a simple society, but they are not easily discerned in our complex economy. *Who* is entitled to *what*, from the dollar which the consumer spends on an automobile? This is an extremely

[14] See Essay v.

complicated and controversial problem, and any decision in practice is likely to rest on semimonopoly power—certainly not on ethical considerations.

5. Altering the distribution of wealth by taxation will not have the same effects as altering distribution before taxes. The former allows the taxpayer to enjoy the prestige which goes with receiving a large income even though he is later obliged to hand over a large portion of that income to the government.

6. The economic consequences of interfering with incentives may change with time and with the expectations of individuals. Income taxes that would have seemed exorbitant forty years ago are now accepted as a necessary feature in the scheme of things.

7. The personal income and death tax rates are much less equalizing than they seem. Much income accumulates in corporations and trusts and is never realized by individuals or is realized only as capital gains that are favored by the tax laws. Many transfers to future generations escape the death tax by the creation of life estates and so forth. The full effect of avoidance and evasion is difficult to appraise but it is undoubtedly very substantial.

Available evidence on the distribution of wealth and income does not suggest that tax laws have leveled high incomes to a point where incentives are unduly threatened. A recent Federal Reserve Board publication showing that, in 1945, ten percent of American families saved sixty percent of all net saving in that year, is not conclusive on the point but it is indicative.[15]

It is fair to say also that a large group of people accept the capitalistic system only on condition that the principal beneficiaries do not require extreme inequalities as ransom for keeping the system going. The group does not go so far as to

[15] *Federal Reserve Bulletin*, Vol. 32, No. 8, Aug. 1946, p. 852.

choose a tax policy deliberately calculated to "soften up the system for the socialist kill." But it has no such love for the existing order that it is willing to call off its program on the charge that it is impeding the successful operation of the system. It has less fear than others that there are no co-operative or socialistic alternatives which can be made to work satisfactorily and without sacrificing basic freedoms. The group is for capitalism but not on the condition that this involves the price of unlimited power and unlimited income for a few leaders.

Just how much people do (as contrasted with should) respond to economic rewards is hard to say. Undoubtedly they differ greatly in this respect. For example, like many other cooperative leaders, the head of the Swedish cooperative movement is apparently content with a very modest salary, preferring the nonmaterial rewards of his present position to the much higher remuneration his administrative talents could command in competitive business. On the other hand, there are university professors who would move to the end of the earth to add $1,000 to their salaries, even though the intangibles associated with their work seemed to favor their remaining where they were. A discouraging datum for the equalizers is the fact that Soviet Russia, contrary to the trends expected in a Marxian state, has inclined more and more in recent years toward incentive payments. Of course, this trend is criticized as a betrayal of socialism and it can be accounted for in terms of a predilection of leadership rather than a necessary concession to the limitations of human nature. The Russians, moreover, do provide a considerable measure of equality in their generous program of social services.

Cynics have always stressed the negative incentive of fear as the only influence which could keep individuals in the "straight and narrow path." Often they have been proved wrong. The case of inequality—especially as it applies to a national minimum of the essentials of life—might be another instance where human nature provides better potential than the cynics expect.

The Possibility of Reducing Inequalities

Questions have been raised, too, as to whether it is possible to obtain greater equality even if we want it. Professor Pareto stimulated much discussion on this subject some years ago when he published an analysis of income distribution in different countries and in the same countries at different times. He observed much the same pattern of income distribution in all of these data.[16] The inference seemed to be that income distribution tends toward a constant pattern regardless of institutional arrangements and that the way to relieve the poor is not to attempt to help them at the expense of the rich but to raise the level of production generally.

Critics, however, have exploded "Pareto's law" quite effectively, although it should be said that Pareto himself laid no claim to have established any "law." Professor Pigou[17] has called attention to the fact that the same institutional framework, in the main, prevailed in all the situations tested by Pareto's data. Particularly important, of course, were the institutions of inheritance and private property, present in all cases.

Pigou has suggested that the underlying reason for a tendency of incomes to assume a constant pattern, if it exists, must be found in a constant scale of biological differences. But biological differences should, and presumably do, follow a bell-shaped curve characteristic of chance variations in natural phenomena. "What meat does Caesar eat that he is so much greater than the rest of us?" The curve suggests that he might be four or five times or even ten times greater but

[16] Vilfredo Pareto, *Manuel d'économie politique*, v, Giard & E. Briére, Paris, 1909.
[17] A. C. Pigou, *Economics of Welfare*, Macmillan, London, 1920. Part v, Chap. II.

certainly not a hundred times greater. If one were to test the length of maple leaves, or the weight of walnuts, or the height of persons, for instance, the results would follow the well-known curve, showing a few dwarfs and a few giants but mostly middle-sized items. (It is well known among instructors, if not among students, that most of those who take an examination are expected to achieve a grade of "C." If this expectation fails to materialize, the instructor will probably conclude that there is something wrong with his examination or his grading. Of course, these are exceptional classes.) The curve of income distribution, on the other hand, is sharply skewed to the right. The "skewness" may measure the effect of institutions, or, as some would say, "special privilege."

Pareto's theory, if true, would support the view that real wages can only be increased, at least for labor as a whole, by increasing output. It would also lend support to the diffusion theory of incidence in public finance. This theory holds that, in the long run, economic forces adjust themselves to the levy of taxes, with the same net effect regardless of the character of the levy. Fortunately, so it seems to the author of these essays, we are not obliged to accept the view that the distribution of income is entirely, or even mainly, beyond the control of mortal man.

Other Species of Equality

Of course, economic equality is only one species of a larger genus. Another species is *biological* equality. That this does not exist outside the philosophy books was long ago established by intelligence tests and, indeed, by simple observation. When the Declaration of Independence says that "all men are created equal" it probably means only that they are entitled to equal treatment. *Legal* equality calls for equal rights in courts of law—a tradition sometimes described as "the fundamental rights of an Englishman." The prince and the pauper are supposed to stand equally before the judge, and even a king might be "fined for speeding." Of course, no one supposes that this form of equality has reached perfect achievement but it is generally approved in theory. *Political* equality calls for equal rights to participate in government regardless of sex, color, or economic status. In some enlightened countries, after many battles, this goal is near achievement. *Social* equality calls for the respectful treatment of all men by each other in their social intercourse. In some parts of the United States social equality is practiced to a degree that amazes foreigners. But we rank low in extending this equality to minorities. Finally, there is *equality of power*. Maldistribution of power may be as much an occasion for concern as maldistribution of income. However, the curse is lifted from such maldistribution if the power is responsible to the ultimate authority of free popular elections.

Equality and Freedom

Philosophers have frequently discussed equality in relation to freedom and have sometimes concluded that there is a conflict between the two objectives. The freedom to retain the fruits of one's labor is sacrificed on the altar of equality. However, the right to a minimum of subsistence is also described as a freedom—in fact, one of "the four freedoms." The issue is complicated by the fact that freedom may consist either of the absence of restraint by government or of the absence of restraint by other circumstances. "A" may be restrained from satisfying his desires because of the tax laws; "B" because of unemployment or ill health. Also there is the complication of whose freedom is being considered. To use a figure of Tawney's: freedom for the pike might mean death to the minnows.[18]

It is evident enough that *equality, economic well-being,* and *freedom from police restraint* are all different though related

18 Tawney, *Equality*, p. 238.

[22]

concepts and values. One may have much of one and little of the others. Thus it may be that there is more equality in Russia than in America, though this is disputed. Certainly the advantage in freedom from police restraint is with us. Napoleon on his desert isle may have been surfeited with bodily comforts and still have lacked any real freedom. A dustbowl farmer in the middle thirties was free to do what he liked (in one sense) but he was "down and out" in his economic status.

Two other concepts complicate the pattern. *Security* is a form of economic well-being but it is also a distinct interest. A dynamic economy might provide a very high standard of living but create many individual economic casualties. This would constitute well-being without security. *The right to participate in government* may attend freedom from police restraint but not necessarily. A property qualification for voting would exclude many citizens from the polls who might otherwise be free to order their lives as they saw fit.

To what extent are these several interests really in conflict? Obviously they compete to some degree. A laissez faire economy offers a minimum of police restraint and possibly also a maximum of economic achievement (although this is disputed) ; its score as to security and equality is very low. A planned economy might offer both security and equality, but it frankly accepts many police restraints (which, say its critics, would end in tyranny).

It is the right to participate in government ("sovereignty rests upon consent") and freedom from police restraint that are strongest in the American tradition. And they are not to be exchanged on easy terms for either more equality or more economic well-being. We have only begun to appreciate the awful potentialities of modern tyranny. It is said that many place a small value on freedom if it means only the freedom to starve. But the alternatives are not usually so extreme as that. Nor need we conclude that a man should sell his soul for

[23]

a full stomach even if he would. The Bible does not praise Esau because he sold his birthright for a mess of pottage. All of the values discussed above are important and it is by no means certain that we cannot have a large measure of each. Insofar as they do compete with each other, the problem is to achieve a balance. Freedom only to starve is intolerable but so also is economic sufficiency and equality in prison.

Conclusion

Does it appear that the tax system has gone too far in the elimination of inequalities? Such evidence as we have concerning the present distribution of wealth and income lends little plausibility to an affirmative conclusion. Indeed, it might be thought to support Pareto's suggestion that equalitarianism is bound to fail. But this, too, would be an unwarranted conclusion both because we do not know what the distribution would have been without the tax system and because the system itself has been at its present and recent levels too short a time for its influence to be fully felt.

While the author supports the view that the tax system has not gone too far (and likely not far enough) in reducing inequalities, he also takes the position that too little heed has been given to the conservation of incentives. Even from the equalitarian's viewpoint, an equalizing program that is skillfully devised can be safely pushed further than one that is clumsy and inept. A tax system that "loads the dice against risk-taking investments of equity capital"[19] should be on the defensive.

However, if the author were confronted with the proposition that graduation in income and inheritance tax rates makes impossible the successful operation of the capitalistic system, his reactions would be: (1) I don't believe it, and (2) if this be true, let us look for a hardier system.

[19] J. M. Clark, "Some *Cleavages* Among Economists," *American Economic Review*, vol. XXXVII, May 1947, p. 3.

This chapter began with the search for a principle which could be used to test the validity of all specific tax measures. The hunt has been none too successful. We rejected per capita division; found grave limitations in the benefit principle; and concluded that ability to pay, while valid as a basis for a tax philosophy with a philanthropic flavor, has no compelling claim upon those who refuse to be philanthropic. At all events, it gives no precise quantitative answers. The equality interest is subject to much the same limitations.

Confronted with this situation, the tax student may abandon the pursuit and turn to a pragmatic test of each particular tax, weighing all of its qualifications and effects against those of available alternatives. This is not too bad a solution but it does not relieve the critic of the necessity of developing and applying a tax philosophy. He will find himself obliged to weigh and balance, for instance, his interest in: (1) the rationality of the tax (that is, the relevance of its distribution to at least some plausible criterion); (2) its effect on inequalities; (3) its economic effects (which will be disputed); and (4) miscellaneous so-called practical aspects, such as ease of collection.

On the other hand, the tax student may select some philosophy as an article of faith. His decision will, of course, depend on his general philosophy of life. With regard to inequalities, people divide themselves into two groups. The first prefers a world in which a free hand is given to the strong and the clever. Wide inequalities do not bother the conscience of this group and are quite congenial to its tastes. Moreover, such inequalities are accepted as necessary economic incentives. The second group holds that the strong have a decided obligation to the weak and stresses the solidarity of human interests. It dislikes and doubts the wisdom of great inequalities. The author belongs in this latter camp.

CHAPTER II
Place of Government
in the Scheme of Things
Introduction

M OST treatises on public finance begin with some discussion of public expenditures and of government's
place in the scheme of things. The relevance of this
subject is obvious: if governments were not so ambitious, the
tax problem could be relatively simple. Moreover, the proper
role of government is of vital consequence in postwar policy
generally. Until recently, at least, nearly every newspaper
brought us reports from Europe of further trends to the
left—and toward more government. Our own people, while
presently committed to end war controls and cut the public
payroll generally, are none too sure of themselves. Thus
an exploration of the sphere of government seems a fitting
task for our second essay.

There are many possible approaches to a study of public
expenditures and the scope of government. One is to consider the effects of public outlay on such aspects of the
economy as production, consumption, and the distribution of
income.[1] Another is to explain the many classifications into
which public expenditure can be divided (such as outlay for
self-liquidating projects versus that for those not self-
liquidating). A further approach is to analyze the principle
of maximum advantage, which tells us that governments
should undertake what they can do more efficiently than
private individuals or groups. A still different tack is to explain the causes for the skyrocket advance in public expenditure. Here one observes the voracious appetite of the war-
making function and concludes that the really big prizes for

[1] Harvey W. Peck, *Taxation and Welfare*, Macmillan, New York, 1925.

the economy-minded lie in the field of international relations; but he also observes that while the state was once conceived to serve mainly as our policeman and warrior, it is now expected to play the role of cooperative, promoter, equalizer, and balance wheel. This leads into the approach here chosen, that of examining the role of the state. Even then one has alternatives: he might delve into political science and philosophy and wrestle with the definition and concept of the state; or he can lead off from an economic angle and examine the role which the state should play in the economy. Being an economist, the author will take the latter of these alternatives.

One's view of the state is coupled so closely with his general economic philosophy that it is possible to consider the two together. Perhaps we can best proceed, therefore, by sketching several economic philosophies of life—and, of course, of the role of government. They are based on different views of what is required to make an economic system function satisfactorily. No claim is made that these categories cover the ground exhaustively. It is recognized that there are many shades of opinion within each philosophy and that an individual can espouse more than one simultaneously.

Deemphasis of Concern for Economic Values

Said John Maynard Keynes: "The economic problem, the struggle for subsistence . . . has been . . . the primary, most pressing problem . . . not only of the human race, but of the whole of the biological kingdom from the beginnings of life in its most primitive forms."[2] There are many, however, who feel that man's preoccupation with wealth-getting—especially beyond the point of subsistence—is unworthy and corrupting. There have been many critics, both at home and abroad, of the so-called overemphasis of materialism in the United States. Thus, Lin Yutang depicts us as ruled by the slogan:

[2] *Essays in Persuasion*, Harcourt, Brace & Co., New York, 1932, p. 366.

[27]

"The greatest goods to the greatest number."[3] André Siegfried went much further to say: "In America, the dominant force that is threatening to carry everything before it, Protestant, Catholic, and Jew is the obsession for tangible and material accomplishment."[4] "It is a materialistic society, organized to produce things rather than people, with output set up as a god."[5] And our own Dorothy Thompson rounds off with: "The world envies our technical and scientific achievements but no country in the world envies or admires the kind of society we have."[6]

These criticisms, though aimed at the United States, could be applied with equal validity to Communist Russia.

The philosopher Henry Thoreau[7] was convinced that poverty, at least voluntary poverty, is not incompatible with the good life and that many spirits are imprisoned by the things they own.

The critics of this alleged overemphasis of economic concern advocate more attention for individuals and less for institutions. Real reform, they hold, must come the Chinese way—by cultivating the moral quality of the individual. Social reform without individual reform is likely to prove a mirage. Says Koestler: "The Second and Third Internationals got into the blind alley because they fought capitalism in its own terms of reference, and were unable to ascend to the spiritual climate the longing for which we feel in our bones."[8]

There is undoubtedly much to be said for the view that a nation can become too prosperous for the good of its own

<hr />

[3] Lin Yutang, *With Love and Irony*, The John Day Co., New York, 1940, p. 21.

[4] André Siegfried, *America Comes of Age*, Harcourt, Brace & Co., New York, 1927, p. 53.

[5] *Ibid.*, p. 348.

[6] Charles A. & Mary R. Beard, *The American Spirit*, Macmillan, New York, 1942, p. 484.

[7] *The Works of Thoreau*, edited by Henry S. Canby, Houghton Mifflin, Boston, 1937, pp. 245-98.

[8] Arthur Koestler, *The Yogi and The Commissar*, Macmillan, New York, 1945, p. 104.

soul. Satisfactory living is more likely to be built upon moral rules and promises faithfully kept than upon economic achievement. The blessings of mass production are very considerably overrated! Prophets who cry out against "the production of goods, more goods, more things, mountains of things—to what purpose?" deserve to be heard. The least we can do in response is to improve the quality of our consumption. *What* we produce should concern us as well as *how much*. Here the government enters, since "socialized consumption" is a main avenue for improving our utilization of wealth.

It seems unlikely, however, that we shall pass up an economy of abundance and further conquests of nature on the ground that they might prove demoralizing. We must somehow learn to live with plenty. Also there is the grim fact of widespread poverty in the midst of much abundance. This poverty, too, is demoralizing. Every social worker knows that along with the bad housing and malnutrition which mark poverty go crime, delinquency, bad health, perverted views, and other ugly social consequences. Economic progress is only one weapon for attacking poverty but it is the one that is least controversial.

Laissez Faire and Individualism

The second philosophy to be considered is based on the view that the economic world is a self-regulating system kept in order by a balance of forces as are the heavenly bodies in the physical universe. Free competition and supply and demand are the economic equivalents of mass and gravitation. Tinkering with the handiwork of providence is likely to prove harmful. Economic laws yield a natural brand of justice; the system tends to distribute to each of the factors of production the amount of wealth it creates. By his pursuit of self-interest the individual unwittingly serves the public good.

This laissez faire doctrine was so well established in 1850

that it could be prescribed without qualification or apology by the Society for Promoting Christian Knowledge.[9] The endorsement included, of course, the idea that men do the greatest service to the public when they are thinking of nothing but their own gain. This identification of economics with self-seeking John Ruskin attacked as a libel upon the businessman.[10] Perhaps the ultimate in the self-interest doctrine was reached by the Supreme Court of Michigan when, in the case of Dodge v. Ford, it sustained the view of minority stockholders that reducing prices and increasing wages is philanthropy rather than business and is beyond the pale of legitimate business policy.[11]

Related to the laissez faire philosophy, but stemming from different roots, is the view of life that may be described as "rugged individualism." One root of this doctrine can be found in Herbert Spencer's adaptation of Darwinism to economics. Growth and progress in both natural and social realms are a matter of survival of the fittest. This view was swallowed whole by Professor William Sumner of Yale, who taught that "without inequality the law of the survival of the fittest could not operate."[12]

Perhaps a more enduring root of individualism can be traced to Puritanism.[13] In the Puritan view, poverty was to be condemned rather than pitied or relieved; a sound whipping

[9] John Maynard Keynes, *Laissez Faire and Communism*, The New Republic, New York, 1926, p. 31.
[10] John Ruskin, *"Unto this Last": Four Essays on the First Principles of Political Economy*, J. Wiley & Son, New York, 1872.
[11] 204 Michigan 459 (1919).
[12] Richard Hofstadter, *Social Darwinism in American Thought*, University of Pennsylvania Press, 1944, p. 44. Carl Snyder is a late proponent of the doctrine of an economic elite to whom is ascribed the main role in economic progress. The miracles of productive power, he says, are mainly the result of placing large accumulations of capital in the hands of a few individuals with rare gifts of management. Avarice and thirst for gain are among the most benevolent forces in the modern world. Future progress is a matter of giving a free hand to the genius population. (Carl Snyder, *Capitalism the Creator*, Macmillan, New York, 1940.)
[13] *Puritanism and Democracy.*

was an appropriate punishment for incorrigible idlers. The rich must regard their wealth as a stewardship and avoid gain at the expense of others; if they met this test they were to be honored. Poor Richard's almanac extols the economic virtues as the Puritans saw them. Even today, success stories make excellent magazine copy. Orison Swett Marden sold his theme of how to get ahead in the world in many books, many editions, and millions of copies.[14] One of the most outstanding and indigenous of America's intellectuals, Ralph Waldo Emerson, is best known for his essay on self-reliance.

The views of the laissez faire proponents and the rugged individualists are vulnerable enough. The laissez faire doctrine took a beating during the thirties when we were confronted by a deep depression which seemed only aggravated by a do-nothing policy. The Spencerian approach has been attacked by John Dewey, among others,[15] on the ground that the unfit may be the antisocial rather than the physically weak or the economically dependent. The businessman often survives by fraud and chicanery rather than by able administration. The Puritan creed gave scant if any recognition to the view that the strong have obligations to the weak—a view increasingly stressed as the conscience of humanity becomes more sensitive.

Yet there surely is something in the old individualism that is worth preserving. Perhaps it is the element which holds that the individual is the object of all social endeavor and only in the degree to which he can develop creatively is a system successful. In these days of much paternalism and statism, when a full stomach for all, however attained, is so frequently exalted as the end product of reform, it is well to recall that it is better to help an individual help himself than only to help an individual.

[14] Merle Curti, *The Growth of American Thought*, Harper, New York, 1943, pp. 649-50.
[15] Hofstadter, *op. cit.*, p. 118.

Moreover, it seems unwise to conclude that we have said farewell entirely to laissez faire. The idea that economic forces can operate with benevolent results, unchecked or unaided by extensive government policing, does seem indeed to have failed the test of experience. However, a coordinated system regulated to follow the design of political leaders may not prove a panacea either. In the second next phase of economic development, at least, we may concentrate our efforts on the achievement of a more successful automatic sphere. We may find, as Walter Lippmann predicts, that government can become too large to be well managed by finite men and that the efforts of intelligent statesmanship once more will be devoted to limiting the role of government. Instead of attempting to reform institutions we may try to develop wisdom in individuals and groups. Certainly it is high time that private business developed a new type of leadership with some understanding and appreciation of the public interest. There are signs that this leadership has begun to appear. It is significant that even Karl Marx envisioned a final stage of evolution in which the state was destined to "wither away," and James Peter Warbasse, intellectual of the cooperative movement, came from a different angle to the same conclusion.

After the above has been said, however, it is still in order to applaud the passing of unbridled individualism. The extremists of laissez faire, such as Herbert Spencer, probably did more to pave the way for socialism and economic planning than the proponents of these philosophies.

The Antimonopoly Philosophy

The antimonopolists are somewhat akin to the individualists but they have a much keener appreciation of the need for positive governmental action to preserve effective competition. Judged by the degree of change they advocate and by their sympathy for the underdog, some of them might be labeled "radical." There is a wide range among them, however, in this respect.

It is said that the soul of a nation can be perceived in its choice of heroes. Perhaps the American statesmen who are honored and revered above all others are Lincoln and Jefferson. The former embodied the American view of the dignity of the common man. Jefferson is identified with that potent strain in American thought and tradition which might be called the antimonopoly philosophy.

Above all else, Jefferson exalted the rural aspect of American life. He had a profound distrust of everything urban including the working class of the cities. Here certainly, he was at the opposite pole from Karl Marx, who distrusted everything rural, referred to farmers as "yokels," and looked forward to the industrialization of agriculture as a prelude for his social revolution. Said Jefferson: "Those who labor in the earth are the chosen people of God, if ever He had a chosen people, whose breasts He has made his peculiar deposit for substantial and genuine virtue."[16]

Jefferson also gave strong support for the strain of anarchy in American thought. It is to this patron saint of liberals that we owe the slogan: "That government is best which governs least."

The antimonopolists fear centralized power, whether exercised by private or public authority. They hold that rich and democratic living requires small and autonomous units whether of school, city or business. They seek a system that aspires to abundant living through the spontaneity of its constituent parts. They may dislike and distrust inequalities and the "money power" quite as much as the socialist, but they are also profoundly skeptical of the latter's propensity for singleness of organization. They see safety and the preservation of values in a plural universe—the maintenance

[16] Charles Beard, *Economic Origins of Jeffersonian Democracy*, Macmillan, New York, 1927, pp. 423-24.

[33]

of alternatives. As one of them puts it: "When I can no longer tell my employer to go to hell and know I can always find another, my kind of a world will have disappeared." For the antimonopolists the federal system is admirably adjusted to the needs of a democratic society; it is a great achievement, one of the greatest "ever struck off by the mind of man." But in our day the central government tends to encroach upon "home rule" mainly because it must control business, which itself has been allowed to grow "too big." Big business has necessitated big labor as well as big government, and the combination seems to be leading us straight to omnipotent statism.

A classic statement of the antimonopolists' fear of bigness is that of Professor Carver:

"If, without the slightest change of character or disposition . . . [the common house cat] were suddenly enlarged to the dimensions of a tiger, we should at least want her to be muzzled and to have her claws trimmed, whereas if she were to assume the dimensions of a mastodon, I doubt if any of us would want to live in the same house with her. And it would be useless to argue that her nature had not changed, that she was just as amiable as ever, and no more carnivorous than she always had been. Nor would it convince us to be told that her productivity had greatly increased and that she would now catch more mice in a minute than she formerly did in a week. We should be afraid . . . that in her large-scale mouse catching she might not always discriminate between us and the mice. . . ."[17] Similarly bigness of a corporation is definitely a matter for the law to take into account.[18]

The growth of chain stores is ordinarily either applauded or accepted with equanimity by a socialist. An antimonopolist may find such a development quite alarming. Justice Brandeis,

[17] Thomas Nixon Carver, *Essays in Social Justice*, Harvard University Press, Cambridge, 1915, p. 332.
[18] *Ibid.*

in his classic dissent in the Florida chain store tax case,[19] expressed the opinion that a legislature may not unreasonably view this centralization of the distribution business as a menace, converting independent tradesmen into clerks and sapping "the resources, the vigor and the hope of the smaller cities and towns."[20]

The antimonopolist rejects the contention that there is an inevitable trend toward concentration in business. He believes that the modern corporation has been allowed to go "hog wild," with no adequate check as to financial structure, business practices, or size. The "trusts" did not evolve out of a natural order; many of them were fostered by discriminations that could and should have been prevented. The government's antitrust division has always suffered from malnutrition, and the courts have given it only halfhearted support. The fact that the same administration could offer N.R.A. and Thurman Arnold in close succession is evidence of the government's vacillation on this vital issue. "The so-called failure of capitalism (of the free enterprise system, of free competition)," wrote Henry Simons, "may reasonably be interpreted as primarily a failure of the political state in the discharge of its minimum responsibilities under capitalism. This view may suggest reasons for skepticism with reference to the currently popular schemes for curing all our ills."[21]

The antimonopolist pins his hopes on such measures as reduced tariffs, federal incorporation, more vigorous antitrust enforcement, and perhaps taxes on size. Improvement of the charters governing private corporations is regarded as an aspect of the economy at once highly neglected and extremely promising.

Although the antimonopolist would like more competition

[19] Louis K. Liggett Co. v. Lee, 288 U.S. 517 (1933).
[20] *Ibid.*, p. 569.
[21] Henry C. Simons, *A Positive Program for Laissez Faire*, Chicago University Press, 1934, p. 4.

[35]

in business, he may also concede that competition is far from a "dead duck." Private enterprise is not hopelessly monopolistic. Indeed, many will argue that competition was never so lively as now. It has been furthered by the development of alternative products. Besides actual current-price competition there is service and quality competition, in addition to potential competition. It is argued that without some check on competition, businesses with high overheads would face chaos. What constitutes "workable competition" under these circumstances has been the subject of much speculation.

The antimonopoly movement has passed its heyday, perhaps, and exercises less influence upon American thought than formerly. Many intellectuals now heap scorn upon it and describe its proponents as reactionaries who would have been liberals had they lived a half century earlier. However, the philosophy is sound in its view that government, along with business, can develop the evils of bigness—arrogance, incoordination, and blindness at the center for the needs at the periphery. It is also sound in its view that there is safety in numbers and richness of living in the spontaneity of men and communities. It remains to be seen if these values are compatible with the equally significant ones of full employment and the progressive elimination of poverty. It is to be fervently hoped that they are. The antimonopoly movement deserves a new birth of vitality.

The Cooperative Movement

Many proponents of the antimonopoly movement are also interested in consumer cooperatives.[22] Some socialists, too, favor the cooperative movement. Nevertheless, the move-

[22] Discussion of the cooperative movement is here confined to consumer-owned industries. Of course, there are also worker-owned industries, a type of development as much related to syndicalism (collective ownership with labor control) as to consumers' cooperation. Then too, there are marketing cooperatives, usually organizations of primary producers who enhance their bargaining power by selling collectively.

[36]

ment has a distinct tradition and philosophy of its own. Many cooperators see in it a check on the growth of the state—a means by which an overgrowth of political power and machinery can be avoided.

The cooperative movement is by no means new in this or other countries but it has only recently grown strong enough here to capture more than passing attention. The movement urges consumers to go into business for themselves. On the foundation of numerous grass-roots local ventures, a superstructure of wholesale and manufacturing business can be developed.

Objectives of consumers' cooperation include, of course, protecting the consumer from the waste and abuses of noncooperative business and from his own ignorance and gullibility. Also included is protection from monopoly. In the United States, the movement, though young, has ventured into the production (directly or under contract) of petroleum products, farm machinery, and tobacco—all monopolistic lines. The movement is also said to be an end in itself—a "way of life."

The cooperative movement lays great stress on the means with which it proposes to accomplish its ends. The means are described as voluntary, peaceful, evolutionary, and democratic. Probably it can truthfully be said that the cooperative movement is the only form of radicalism which involves no social risks whatever.

Perhaps the limitations of the movement are related to this lack of risk. The achievements of cooperation develop slowly, and feverish radicals are likely to feel that reform will not wait so long. Business administration may be simpler and easier under autocratic than under democratic auspices. Quite frequently those most interested in the cooperative movement do not have the capital required for rapid expansion, and even though the movement is mature in Europe, it has made little attempt to invade the heavy industries there. Nevertheless,

[37]

the cooperative movement appeals to many as the golden mean between the excesses of capitalism on the one hand and the dangers of socialism on the other. The least to be said for the movement is that it provides a valuable alternative for monopoly capitalism. Freedom in no small part consists of the availability of effective alternatives.

If the farm-machinery trust holds up prices and is slow to adopt new ideas, as alleged, let the farmers produce their own tractors and milking machines. If the manufacturers of razor blades deliberately use poor steel in order to sell their wares, let the consumers themselves prove this. If the tobacco trust is knee-deep in unjust enrichment, let the consumers try their hand at producing and distributing cigarettes. Of course, the road is not easy, but one is entitled to hope that not all the courage and skill are on the side of the monopolists. At least, the road for alternative forms of organization should be kept as open as possible.

Socialism

Not all socialists are Marxists, but all have been influenced considerably by the intellectual stimulation and leadership of Karl Marx. We cannot attempt here to explain his famous doctrines: the economic interpretation of history; surplus value; class struggle; growing concentration of industry; increasing severity of crises; progressive misery of the exploited classes; inevitable revolution, with the state falling heir to the important means of production; dictatorship of the proletariat; and ultimate economic democracy with a decreasing role for the state. Very few accept this body of doctrine today without qualification: some consciously accept it with qualification; and many more borrow from it unconsciously. One writer sizes up Marx's contribution with the observation that whatever may have been the blind spots in his doctrine, he was "irresistibly right in his prophecy that the civilization of his epoch was built upon the sand."[23] Socialists would add that the foundation has improved little, if any, since his time.

Among the weaknesses and contradictions in present-day capitalism, stressed by socialists, is the unemployment of men and resources. The chronic tendency toward unemployment might be disputed but at least, it is said, the wave motion known as the business cycle represents a cross which capitalism—and only capitalism—has to bear. The only sovereign remedy for unemployment yet devised by the democracies is total war. While we have relied on competition to control prices, the large-scale business corporation has developed and it is the acme of irresponsible power. An attempt to atomize these corporations would be only trying to make the clock run backward. Increasing cynicism and distrust, it is argued, are manifest on all sides. The complications of our uncoordinated economic system and its unheralded gyrations have proved too much for even professional economists to explain, and probably to understand. Monetary and fiscal reforms seeking stabilized full employment are inflationary and opportunistic. Since the early days, at every crisis a host of soft-money cranks have appeared, offering to save a rotten institutional structure by pumping in credit. When will we learn that the patient requires a more fundamental operation?

Defenders of capitalism are frequently unimpressed by these charges. They cite the impressive record of achievement which capitalism has to its credit. Taking the offensive, they point to an alleged blindness of their opponents to the dangers and difficulties in a greatly enlarged political sphere. Here they have on their side the long-standing American distrust of government. They point out that the President and Congress are already overloaded and that the level of

[23] Harry W. Laidler, *Social-Economic Movements*, Thomas Y. Crowell Co., New York, 1944, pp. 158-59; direct quote is from Harold J. Laski, *Karl Marx, An Essay*, League for Industrial Democracy, New York, 1933.

personnel manning the elected branches of our federal, state, and municipal governments is none too high. Says Schumpeter: "No responsible person can view with equanimity the consequences of extending the democratic method, that is to say, the sphere of 'politics,' to all economic affairs."[24]

Socialism is, of course, a matter of degree as indicated by the fact that our present economic order is often described as a "mixed economy." Quite possibly evolution may take the form of enlarging the portion of government ownership in the mixture. As attractive precedent for this trend, Sweden is often cited. Anticipating a later discussion, we may observe that a mixed economy of the Swedish type has an important strategic advantage in its control of business cycles. In such an economy, public investment for compensatory purposes may take the form of expansion in the capital and equipment of public industries. A common criticism of self-liquidating public works as a depression measure is that there are not enough prospective works to counteract unemployment. Sweden need have less concern than some other countries on this score. The commonly accepted rule that governments should undertake what they can perform more efficiently than private enterprise is satisfactory only if the term efficiency is construed to include all the social results. Under this rule one can often make a plausible and convincing case for the expansion of government ownership and operation in the area of public utilities and some natural resources.

It is also true that collective ownership is open to a variety of institutional forms. The Tennessee Valley Authority, rather than the post office, might serve as a model of a public corporation. A mixed corporation, with the government exercising a majority vote in the control, has possibilities. These alternatives are not necessarily incompatible with the antimonopolist's hope of maintaining a pluralistic universe.

[24] Joseph A. Schumpeter, *Capitalism, Socialism, and Democracy*, Harper, New York and London, 1942, p. 299.

The socialists have scored impressive gains in Europe and their program seems much less remote and unattainable in America than it once did. The pragmatic progressive who has constituted the traditional opposition to the *status quo* in this country has never taken to the "isms." But Americans do insist that their economic system shall make progress against the age-old problems of unemployment and poverty. Looking toward the future they will insist on rapid progress, for popular articles on the potentialities of the new technology have taken hold. The typical American now has his fingers crossed regarding the economics of the future. He would prefer progress along familiar roads involving no risk of traditional values. However, if these roads become blocked and lead only to frustration, the socialists might yet have their day.[25]

Over-all Planning

There is an alternative to socialism little if any less inviting to the opponents of capitalism and one that might prove more attractive to the American people. It is known as "over-all economic planning." The planners agree with the socialists that steady economic progress is not to be expected from *uncoordinated* private production. However, the socialists are wrong, it is said, in their view that collective ownership is necessary to achieve coordination. Control is the meat of ownership; the government has already helped itself to some of this meat and it can take more. Our economy is impressive in many respects but it lacks direction. Thus, says George Soule: "We have magnificent muscles in our great industrial plants; efficient arteries in our railroads and highways; sensitive nerves in our lines of communication. But we

[25] Nothing is said here about the communists, who differ from the less radical socialists, among other respects, in their willingness to sacrifice civil rights to attain their ends.

have only a trace of gray matter in our economic cranium."[26]
Planning looks moderate but it can have radical implications;
what the planners propose to do in effect is to leave the body
of private enterprise in Detroit and Pittsburgh but take the
soul to Washington. Growing concentration in industry is an
open invitation to over-all planning. A large part of the economic system could be brought under control with a very few
orders. Let it be shown that "the two hundred" corporations
have deliberately chosen to restrict output for their own good
and at the expense of the public and the private character of
these companies could disappear quickly. Again it may be
observed parenthetically that the "wave of the future" may
be in the area of mixed control of the corporate institution.

In some respects the planners are considerably more radical
than the socialists. When the time is ripe to center all important authority in the federal government, they intend "to
act fast." Alfred Bingham, in his advice to planners, observes
that "you can't jump over a ditch by a series of short tenta-
tive jumps."[27]

Just how far the planners would have to go in achieving
coordination is discussed with frankness and discernment
by Mrs. Barbara Wootton in her *Freedom Under Planning*.
Cultural freedom must and can be preserved. It is possible "to
coordinate the time tables of the different railway lines without controlling the topics of conversation inside the car-
riages."[28] Freedom of choice may also be allowed in consumption and vocation. On the other hand, prices and wages
would need to be controlled and labor unions would have to
accept this fetter. Mrs. Wootton would be the last to contend

[26] George Soule, *A Planned Economy*, Macmillan, New York, 1932,
p. 60.
[27] Alfred M. Bingham, *Man's Estate*, W. W. Norton, New York, 1939,
p. 379.
[28] Barbara Wootton, *Freedom Under Planning*, University of North
Carolina Press, Chapel Hill, 1945, p. 27; direct quote is from Karl
Mannheim, *Diagnosis of Our Times*, p. 103.

that even the lowest income recipients have nothing to lose but their chains. She concedes that the program would require long-term commitments and hopes that all political parties might agree eventually to inaugurate such a step.

The planners in this country are now in full retreat following the death and burial of O.P.A. However, if and when the time comes for another W.P.A. with its wasteful utilization of labor resources, the alternative of planned production of essential goods and services—the "organization principle" —is sure to prove attractive.

Partial Planning Through Fiscal and Monetary Policy

Some would draw no distinction between over-all planning and so-called fiscal planning. Others espouse fiscal planning as a means of avoiding wholesale regimentation and at the same time of ensuring adequate employment opportunity. The state, says Sir William Beveridge, is in a different position from private citizens in that it can control *money* rather than be controlled by it.

The economic doctrine of the fiscal-control philosophers is largely the work of John Maynard Keynes.[29] Keynes attacked the traditional doctrine that unemployment is due to excessive wages—to labor "pricing itself out of the market." He also attacked the traditional view that the volume of saving and investment is nicely adjusted by a fluctuating interest rate. Reducing wages during a period of unemployment might aggravate rather than relieve the problem. Automatic changes in the interest rate might not occur nor lead to full employment if they did. Saving and investment will be brought into balance instead, perhaps, through a curtailment of the national income, which in turn affects the ability to save. The real cause of unemployment is the fact that the propensity to consume and invest runs short of the propensity to save. The

[29] John Maynard Keynes, *The General Theory of Employment, Interest and Money*, Harcourt, Brace, New York, 1936.

[43]

problem is one of money flow. The real remedy must be found in augmenting either consumption or investment.

However, there are many ways to augment "outlay." Beveridge lists five points at which consumption or investment might be expanded: (1) private investment; (2) private consumption; (3) subsidized private consumption (such as food subsidies); (4) public investment in public business (such as government utilities); (5) socialized consumption (government outlays for public services). In periods of unemployment, outlay might be encouraged by expanded public expenditures financed with deficits; by expanded public expenditures financed by progressive taxes; or by reduced taxes (expenditures remaining constant).[30]

Of course, we must distinguish between cyclical and chronic unemployment. It has long been recognized that fluctuation in outlay for new capital and inventory is one of the factors that generate the ups and downs in business and employment. Many Keynesians, going further, contend that there is a persistent tendency in a rich and highly industrialized country toward oversaving and underinvestment or underconsumption. This so-called stagnant-economy thesis is usually associated with Professor Alvin Hansen,[31] who argues that declining investment is due to a decreasing rate of population growth, the passing of the frontier, a dearth of great new industries, and the increasing ability of business to finance itself by depreciation reserves and reinvested earnings. All of Hansen's fears are belittled by his critics, especially George Terborgh,[32] who argues that population trends and the closing of the frontier are by no means new phenomena nor is there any evidence that industries are more able now than formerly

[30] William H. Beveridge, *Full Employment in a Free Society*, W. W. Norton, New York, 1945, pp. 142-46.

[31] Alvin H. Hansen, *Fiscal Policy and Business Cycles*, W. W. Norton, New York, 1941.

[32] George Terborgh, *The Bogey of Economic Maturity*, Machinery and Other Allied Products Institute, Chicago, 1945.

THE PLACE OF THE GOVERNMENT

to finance their own needs. As for new industries, no one knows what inventions may be knocking at the door and, moreover, many small innovations may be as effective in absorbing capital as a few large ones.

No doubt there is wisdom to be had from a study of economic history but its lessons are far from apparent and unambiguous. It is argued with plausibility that oversaving and excessive profits caused the depression of 1929 and with equal plausibility that deficit spending, when given a trial during the thirties, was a failure. It is also argued that the late twenties were characterized by overinvestment, that is, by overdevelopment of productive capacities in relation to the prospective market. Of course, we had had severe depressions before, even when income levels were lower and when investment opportunities were apparently more abundant.

The fear of oversaving is based largely on deductive analysis which suggests, at least plausibly, that a static economy could absorb little if any saving. Replacements would appear in the accounts as costs, before net income was totaled. Saving is required to finance an *expansion* of demand and to develop innovations. The innovations also result in some loss of old capital. The rate of innovation may vary to some extent fortuitously, to some extent according to the institutional environment. A rich economy will insist on saving substantially whether or not there is any demand for new capital. The conclusions are: (1) that a dynamic and progressive economy is essential to full employment in a rich country, and (2) that public policy should be set to a mold that either discourages saving or promotes its absorbents. This doctrine is not verified by enough experience or evidence to justify unlimited confidence; but it does have sufficient plausibility to justify a public policy framed accordingly, especially since such policy would be in harmony with other social interests.

Let us return to the problem of coping with the business cycle. Obviously this is a large order and our treatment must

[45]

necessarily be extremely sketchy. During the twenties the favorite tools of the stabilizers were in the realm of central banking policy—rediscount rates, open-market operations, changing reserve requirements, and the like. The central banks were expected to check booms by making it more difficult for commercial banks to lend, reversing this procedure when times were bad. These tools are still valued and many would make them more effective now by raising reserve requirements substantially and by counting government securities held by banks as reserves. This would help to restore to the federal government its power of control over "credit money." But such controls are much weakened by the fact that private loans now account for only a minor part of the assets of commercial banks.

More popular currently is the proposed use of taxation to check expansion and contraction. Taxation can influence the Keynesian "propensities" in two ways: the general level at which purchasing power is shunted into the treasury will affect the ability to spend and invest; and the distribution of taxes among taxpayers (upper and lower brackets) will affect all the factors—spending, investment, and saving.

Historically, taxation has seldom if ever been used as a device to control business cycles. The policy has been to lower taxes when times were good and revenue easy to raise and then to "get tough" when conditions reversed themselves. Such, with qualifications, was our procedure during the twenties and thirties. Now the proposal is to give the government a compensatory role. It is expected to be optimistic, so to speak, when private business is pessimistic, and vice versa. Some would go only so far as to try to stabilize tax rates, allowing tax yields to fluctuate with cyclical trends. Others recommend the bolder course of applying lower effective rates when the base itself drops.

The ultimate in the conception of taxation as a fiscal-control device has been expressed by Abba P. Lerner[33] as follows: "The purpose of taxation is never to raise money but to leave less in the hands of the taxpayer." "The government can raise all of the money it needs by printing it if the raising of money is the only consideration." Those who suppose that taxation exists to provide a meal ticket for government are simply behind the times!

The idea of using taxation as a countercycle control has not gone unchallenged. There are those, Professor Lutz, for instance, who believe that the budget should be balanced every year or at least that a break-neck effort should be made toward this end. They hold that a cyclical budget, in practice, will be all deficits and no surpluses and that this will inevitably lead to an ever-mounting national debt and inflation. They reject the idea that inflation of prices will wait until we reach full employment.

As previously suggested, the business cycle is the great conundrum of capitalism, and so far we have made little progress in getting it under control. We can afford to reject no device that is at all promising. At the very least, we might try keeping the rates of taxation stable while the tax base fluctuates over the cycle.

In a sense, taxation and public expenditure are but opposite sides of the shield. Instead of or in addition to tax measures to cope with deflation, we could inaugurate public spending or public investment. Compensatory spending or investment encounters the difficulty that unless it is so done as not to shake business confidence, it continually enlarges the deflationary gap with one shovel while it fills in with another. The psychological factors in business recovery are extremely important, and no one stressed this more than John Maynard Keynes. Some of this circular motion was in process, perhaps, during the thirties.

[33] Abba P. Lerner, *The Economics of Control*, Macmillan, New York, 1944, p. 307.

Two things might be done to increase the effectiveness of compensatory spending. One is monetary education; businessmen still remain who are not convinced that it is one thing for the government to go into the red (as a monetary measure) and quite another for a state or individual to do so. The second is to set up a public investment program so creative in character that it can be paid for out of fees and a future improvement in the tax base. This would put the expanding productive debt of the government in the same class with expanding bank loans.

The following ten tenets supported by some Keynesians, either directly or by implication, may be listed in conclusion. The first five seem tenable to the author but he is skeptical of the last five:

1. It is possible for a nation to save too much; that is, to overindulge in thrift.

2. This would mean an obstruction in money flows; quite possibly depression and unemployment; quite certainly a lowering of national income.

3. In a rich and highly developed country, a shortage of markets is likely to be more of a problem in the long run than a shortage of goods. We are much more likely to encounter unemployment relief than rationing.

4. When a tax-rate adjustment is being contemplated, important consideration should be given to its effect on inflation and deflation.

5. Governments from now on will be forced inevitably into the assumption of responsibility for the unemployed; if these governments do not spend beyond their current means during a severe depression in order to promote a revival, they will and should do so anyhow to make life bearable for the unemployed.

6. The relationships between spending, saving, investment, and income are very inelastic and do not change substantially

over even long periods of time; oversaving, accordingly, is certain and inevitable except as it is corrected by government action.

7. A proper interpretation of recent economic history leads to the conclusion that the thirties are typical of what we can expect in the future.

8. It is possible and desirable for governments to discount unemployment in advance, so to speak, and thus prevent it from ever appearing.

9. There can be no inflation and rise in prices until our human and other resources are fully employed.

10. One can prove a thesis so completely by deductive logic that he can rest assured thereafter of having all the answers.

Conclusion

In concluding this essay, we observe first that the state seems destined to play a very large role in the immediate future, no matter who wins elections. Several economic philosophies of life are competing for adherents. In addition to these is the pragmatic tradition of the American people. It rightly insists that we make rapid progress against the age-old problems of poverty and unemployment but commits itself to no dogma as to how this must be done. The author has indicated his preference for a mixed economy, which leaves a large sphere to self-governing forces (free enterprise plus cooperatives), but he has emphasized that in our day this means positive program and not a mere abnegation of government. Public ownership and operation in the zone of public utilities and some natural resources are often desirable on direct analysis and may have further advantage as an outlet for compensatory investment. Almost any experimentation, not clearly incompatible with democracy, is preferable to chronic unemployment. Our progress in understanding the business cycle is not a cause for self-congratulation among economists: at present, some of the Keynesian (compensatory) tools are the best we have and should be applied accordingly.

All of this may seem to involve some hedging and compromise and opportunism; but then again it may be common sense. The pragmatic tradition is the dearest and best established of any we have in America.

CHAPTER III
The Future Role of the Net Income Tax
Introduction

THE two previous essays have dealt with over-all aspects of public finance and the final chapter returns to this theme. Chapter III constitutes a digression in that it treats certain problems of a specific tax—the net income tax. Starting with the degree of emphasis that should be given this tax in the postwar federal revenue system, we shall be on ground not far removed from over-all problems. The aspects of net income taxation selected for further discussion—namely, exemptions, personal versus corporate taxation, averaging, and the broader aspects of administration—are all closely related to the over-all picture. Chapter IV is also to some extent a digression. It treats comparatively some of the major taxes available for state and local purposes.

Selecting a Major Tax for the Postwar Federal Tax System

The selection of a leading tax in a tax system must, of course, be related to the conditions of time and place. One would not recommend the income tax for a major role in present-day China where three-quarters or more of the population are engaged in farming, much of it for subsistence rather than for the market. (The income tax works well only for income passing through the market and its application to the imputed incomes of the self-sufficing economy has always been incomplete and imperfect.) Moreover, in China inadequate capital rather than insufficient markets is the major problem. Nor would one suggest the income tax for first choice in Soviet Russia, where the distribution of income is a matter of political control and where the maintenance of an adequate market for goods is clearly no problem.

In an economy where the government is the major entrepreneur, the tax problem is an entirely different species from the one we know. Price and tax policy are so intermingled as to be almost indistinguishable. Neither would the income tax have been recommended for an important role in this country in 1870. The economy was much more agricultural then than now and farmers were much more self-sufficient. The developing West ensured an outlet for new capital. The practice of accounting, now widely applied and greatly refined, was then in its infancy. (It is an open question whether the income tax owes more to the accounting profession or the reverse!) Moreover, the citizenry was not yet schooled in its responsibilities toward government. Whatever else may be said about the recent wars, they have been a first-class lesson in discipline for taxpayers. The British, with their high proportion of industrial wage earners among the gainfully employed and with their long cultivation of civic discipline, provide the environment where the income tax can be given greatest play. However, the environment contemplated for postwar America is sufficiently favorable to warrant a distinctly prominent place for the net income tax.

Why the Income Tax Merits First Choice

There are several reasons why the net income tax appears to be a "natural" for a major role in the tax system of postwar America. In the first place, it is a rational way to raise revenue. All taxes (with a few exceptions) come out of income eventually and a presumption favors taking them out directly and in some consistent proportion to what there is to tax. Why approach taxpayers indirectly, for instance, according to the number of mechanical refrigerators they buy? Surely this item on consumers' budgets bears no consistent relationship to what there is to pay taxes with nor is it relevant to any relationship between taxpayers and the government. Cash and not refrigerators is the medium in which we pay our taxes.

The rationality of the income tax holds up well, too, after we have examined its incidence. Better than most other taxes, it stays put, or remains with those who pay it in the first instance. Because the tax is imposed upon the individual in his role as citizen, is based on the totality of income, and is differentiated among recipients, its effect upon the price structure is probably negligible.

Rationality in the tax system may not always be preferred by the public, influenced as the latter is by nonrational or irrational appeals; but a rational critic is obliged to prefer a reasonable to an arbitrary or capricious distribution of the tax load.

The net income tax as now collected (with current payment and withholding) is probably the most flexible element in the tax system. It can be altered at relatively short notice to meet the needs of inflation and deflation. Without any change in the tax law itself, the drain of purchasing power into the treasury adjusts itself automatically to countercycle requirements. It is true, of course, that the income tax may have a dampening effect on the incentive to invest. In this respect, something will depend on the kind of income tax selected. One with a broad base, with due moderation in its graduation, and with due allowance for losses, need not have serious effects on incentives. No doubt the death tax is better adapted to the dual objectives of promoting wide markets and maintaining incentives. It can be given an enlarged role in the postwar tax system, but the fact that in the main it strikes transfers from one generation to another severely limits its potential base and its revenue possibilities. The other taxes in the tax system—consumption taxes and property taxes—probably have a perverse effect upon the market; they bear with greater weight relatively on the poor than on the rich.

The income tax is also conducive to the production of goods having a high social importance—goods socially preferable to more gadgets and possibly more leisure.

Of course, the income tax is the revenue source best adapted to equalitarian objectives (discussed in Essay 1). Even if graduation be moderate and personal credits conservative, the influence of the tax will be on the side of less inequality. In this respect it contrasts sharply with almost all other taxes.

On the negative side, it is true that there are administrative and political difficulties in income taxation. We have not yet demonstrated that we can apply a direct tax with high rates to large numbers of low-income farmers, professional men, and individual businessmen. Nor have we demonstrated the discipline to maintain the breadth of base and the high effective rates necessary to make a direct tax supply most of our revenue needs. There is now and always has been a battle between opportunism and rationality in taxation, and a complete victory for rationality would be too much to expect. But the federal government has never really *tried* to administer a mass income tax. As we grow more civilized, with civic virtues and accounting practices responding to intensive cultivation, we may expect a distinct trend toward rationality in taxation.

Breadth of Base

There are income taxes and income taxes, however, and the next question to consider is what kind we should have. Most income taxes, as we know them, allow a personal credit for family living expenses. Our federal law now (1947) allows the taxpayer $500 for himself and an additional $500 for each dependent. Besides this, at least ten percent of income is allowed for deductions, such as contributions and personal taxes. Thus, a family of six gets personal exemptions, in effect, of $3300.

The case for not taxing low incomes rests soundly on the

idea that providing public luxuries at the expense of private necessities is poor economics. In other words, there could hardly be a defense for levying taxes that compelled low-income recipients to live in hovels while monumental public buildings were being constructed. Since taxes are not ordinarily earmarked, this analysis requires us to compare the least justifiable of our public expenditures with the most important private wants sacrificed because of tax collections. Much governmental outlay would stand up under this test. For instance, reasonable expenditure for protection could be supported even though it took the food from the tables of underprivileged families. But by no means could all governmental expenditures be so classified.

However, the analysis is much complicated by the fact that the *practical* choice may not lie between more expenditure and less income tax. It may be instead between more income tax and more some-other-kind-of-tax, or between a service very important to the small taxpayer and less income tax.

Only a limited amount of revenue can be had from the high brackets of income no matter how severely they are treated. The issue seems thus reduced to a choice between weighting the load on the upper middle class and increasing the coverage of the lower middle class (it being assumed that the very poorest will be exempt in any case). As a matter of economic analysis, one would conclude for the narrower tax. But again, viewed realistically, this may not be the choice. The alternative to a rational and progressive levy applied to the masses may be a sales tax, which hits them even harder and which is generally less equitable. Perhaps the answer is to raise income tax exemptions only after other obnoxious taxes that adversely affect the lower incomes are repealed. This would put the matter in its proper perspective.

Moreover, taxation is a branch of political science as well as of economics. In political science we learn that many jurisdictions require some ownership of property as a condition for voting (at least in local elections). This restriction is properly regarded as a survival from a less democratic era. Nevertheless, the practice is not entirely indefensible. Citizens probably do vote more responsibly when they have an equity in the consequences. All government is in some degree a case of spending other people's money; but there is some warrant for minimizing this characteristic.

There are other arguments supporting the view that income tax exemptions usually err on the side of overgenerosity and that the tax base should be kept broad. The potential yield of the tax, both as to amount and stability, will depend substantially upon the breadth of its coverage. Were income tax exemptions raised to the point advocated by some critics, the federal tax base would be reduced to a level where even confiscatory rates could not possibly satisfy the treasury's needs.

Taxpayers' morale is adversely affected if only a small number are required to finance exclusively the benefits of governmental services voted by the masses. Morale, even of the large taxpayer, is not to be lightly squandered. Many wealthy taxpayers are public-spirited citizens; witness their substantial contributions to philanthropies. They do resent being "shaken down" and "played for suckers" by taxes to which most of the voters have contributed no equity.

Equalitarians are often criticized on the ground that they are enthusiastic about a "share-the-wealth" program only so far as it applies to ranges of income above their own. Cited as an example is a person who contends that those having two automobiles should share one but that the same principle should not apply to those having two shirts, the reason being that this particular person *has* two shirts. A proper test of the sincerity of equalitarians is their willingness to see their creed applied over a wide range of incomes, including their own.

Probably low-income groups are ill-advised to oppose a

broad-based income tax. The principle of graduation ensures, of course, that those with low incomes will pay relatively less than those above them in the economic scale. Wide participation in financing important social services reduces opposition to their extension. On the other hand, it must always be remembered that the "opportunity cost" (the value of the private expenditure made impossible by the tax) is high when low incomes are included in the tax base.

It is argued for high personal exemptions that they are in accord with the ability-to-pay theory and are required for the consistent application of the income tax. They are conceived as an allowance for the maintenance of the breadwinner; until he has enough to keep him and his family in a state of physical and moral efficiency, there really is no receipt of net income. Thus the allowance is analogous to that provided the businessman for the maintenance of his capital. The allowance is thought of as an expense of doing business rather than as a provision for consumption. The exemption credits are often compared with the cost-of-living figures compiled and published by government bureaus. If the exemptions are below the cost of living, they should be raised.

This line of argument is persuasive but not entirely valid. Subtractions from the income tax base are allowed partly to recognize *relative* differences in ability to pay. The deduction of expenses for the maintenance of capital is thus mainly justified. If "A" and "B" make the same income except that "A" depletes his capital substantially and "B" does not, there is a difference between the two incomes that should be recognized. A true parallel does arise in the personal allowances for the family man as compared with those for taxpayers without dependents. The analogy supports a generous allowance for dependents but not for the taxpayer himself.

The cost-of-living calculations are related to time and place and are usually in excess of the requirements for *physical* maintenance. As civilization advances, more goods are continually added to those classed as conventional necessities. In other words, a cost-of-living index tends to gravitate toward the average income of the country. It may be both desirable and necessary to collect some direct taxes from those with incomes below the average. Then too, account must be taken of the fact that many necessities of life are supplied by the government.

Of course, the pressures of politics are all against a broad-based income tax. Even conservative politicians usually deem it expedient to promise and deliver a more generous allowance for living expenses. The broad-based tax strikes large numbers of voters and they are sensitive to direct taxes. A sales tax is much easier to "put over." But here again the disinterested critic is obliged to choose rationality in taxation even though he hardly expects to be sustained at the polls. He should pay respect to the high "opportunity cost" involved in taxing low incomes *by any tax*, but he should be wary about boarding the bandwagon for higher income tax exemptions.

Graduation

As indicated in Essay I, substantial graduation is accepted by the author as a desirable feature of postwar income taxation. It was concluded that the reduction of inequalities in the United States by means of the tax system has erred on the negative rather than on the positive side. The exact scale that would be appropriate to achieve the desirable reduction of inequalities need not here be considered. Much would depend upon the prevailing circumstances—particularly the elimination of tax loopholes. The latter are far more important to the equalitarian objective than high rates.

Personal versus Corporate Income Tax

A second major question in determining the kind of income tax to feature in the postwar tax system is whether the

[58]

tax should be applied to business (particularly corporate business) as such. Here the American practice (the United States and Canada) differs from the British. The British tax on corporations is mainly a collection at the source from stockholders, who are allowed a credit for the tax paid on their behalf. In America, corporations are taxed as such, with no credit allowed the stockholders.

The corporation is a person, legally speaking, and neutrality might seem to require the same treatment for all persons, natural and legal. Some income tax laws have applied the same graduation scale to both. Of course, when it comes to exemptions, corporations have no dependents—unless their subsidiaries be counted as such. But surely this procedure in general is irrational. It takes no account of: (1) that corporate net incomes may represent different ratios of earnings to invested capital; (2) that some corporations are widely and others closely held; and (3) that possibly some of the corporate tax can be passed along to consumers or wage earners. A small corporate income may represent more prosperity and be more attractive than a large one if the former represents a higher ratio of profits to capital. A stockholder might reasonably prefer being "a large frog in a small puddle" to the reverse. And what becomes of neutrality anyway if the tax is passed on?

The tax on corporations is more rational, perhaps, when not graduated, but it is not easy to defend in any case. Let us assume for the moment that the incidence (final burden) is on the stockholders and their potential dividends. This means that two taxes are levied on profits where only one applies to bond interest and salary income (both of the latter are deductible in arriving at corporate net income). It should be remembered that the double tax represents a qualitative and not a quantitative distinction. This is not a case of assessing a $25,000 income relatively higher than a $5,000 income, but of assessing $25,000 from profits more than $25,000 from interest. It can be argued, of course, that there is a moral difference between the two which justifies the distinction. The view is taken that all business is more or less a racket anyhow. Unfortunately, there is more basis for this conviction than one would wish. But probably the salary paid the manager of a racketeering business is as immoral as the profits paid to stockholders. The fact that the profit income is non-contractual and contingent hardly gives it a moral inferiority. We are not prepared to say that the farmer's income is morally inferior to that of his hired man. Although there are many rackets connected with business, other fields, including even religion, are not immune.

It can be argued, too, that the government is the silent partner in the earning of business profits and that the silent partner is entitled to his pay as taxes. Where would business be without government? But where would any of us be? The silent partner is a factor in all income, wherever earned or by whom.[1] More plausibly it is contended that business is no longer well controlled by competition and makes monopoly profits which can be recaptured by a corporate tax. However, even labor unions do not function strictly according to the rule book of pure competition. While the workingman's "take" from infractions of the rules is usually small per capita, so also is his tax when all incomes pass through the graduated personal income tax mill. Nearly all incomes in our type of society are based on economic power, and it seems hard to improve upon the quantitative classification provided by the personal tax system.

While it seems probable that most of the corporate tax comes out of rewards otherwise destined for stockholders, it is by no means certain that the full incidence is upon them all of the time. It is generally agreed that shifting the corpo-

[1] Moreover, would corporations vote for the present volume of public services were the decision theirs and were the issue one of private investment?

rate tax is distinctly easier and more probable than passing on the personal tax. An old rule of incidence doctrine tells us that a tax on surplus (return above costs) cannot be shifted. However, it is not clear in this rule whether costs include an element of "necessary profits," subject to the corporate tax. Another rule is that prices are set by the cost of the most expensive portion of the supply—that provided by the marginal concern. But there is also a time-honored doctrine which holds that prices must cover the profits that go to a "representative company." In the case of monopoly, the important rule is that a tax on net earnings will not change the monopoly price or the volume of production at which profits are maximum. Intangible factors, however, such as the threat of potential competition, may qualify even this rule.

But it is denied by some that conventional incidence theory has any relevance when a tax is general; in this case, it is said, that incidence blends with more remote effects. The effects of the tax must be traced through its bearing on aggregate demand or through what happens to consumption, savings and investment. If inadequate demand is the limiting factor in production and if the corporate tax would affect aggregate demand less adversely than other alternatives then the conclusion follows that the tax makes for full employment, all-out production, and the desirable social consequences that attend these phenomena. It is argued that no general tax, be it the corporation tax or a general sales tax or any other levy, can be said to affect the consumer directly through an increase in production costs or a decrease in the supply of production factors. The fallacy is said to arise because a theory that was designed for explaining the consequences of a tax on a particular product (and has valid application in this limited sphere) is applied to the universe.

It is probably true that the effects of a universal tax are far more complex than traditional theory explains. But taking a long view, one finds it hard to believe that a tax which increases costs of production factors or limits their supply will not ultimately raise costs of consumers goods. It may be true that some of the costs will be diffused among the various rewards of the factors of production. But at any event a high cost country is likely to afford less real income to its people than a low cost country. It seems unlikely that the Hobsonian distinction between taxes on costs and taxes on surpluses is due for complete extinction.

The rationality of a tax depends in no small degree upon the dependability of its incidence.

Of course, any objection to the double taxation of profits does not hold for the portion of corporate earnings not distributed. Rational procedure clearly does not sanction subjecting distributed earnings to the rigorous treatment of the personal tax system and letting undistributed earnings go free of personal tax, at least until such time as they are eventually divided. The most rational form of corporate taxation is thus a levy on undistributed profits.

It is true that most businessmen are allergic to the idea of an undistributed profits tax. They had some experience with a measure of this species beginning in 1936 and the verdict was "never again!" The 1936 law was inaugurated under unhappy circumstances and was not a very refined instrument. It was ushered out, following the recession of 1937, with too little regard for the fact that the problem it sought to solve remained on our doorstep.

It can be argued that so long as business provides employment and income, why worry about current taxes? The personal income tax will catch up with undistributed income when the stockholder dies or sells out of his company. The earnings that have accumulated will make his stock more valuable and the increment will appear as personal income in the form of a capital gain. Unfortunately, at least for this solution, capital gains (including increments realized on the transfer of securities) are taxed at half (and in some cases, less than half) rates, and those passed on to an heir are wiped out entirely.[2] Of course, these favors could (at least theoretically) be eliminated.

However, time is important in taxation and it seems inequitable to let undistributed earnings escape some immediate equivalent of the personal tax. Obviously, no simple and perfect solution is possible. The author has suggested elsewhere that we might take a leaf from the British here and collect at the source the equivalent of a low-bracket personal tax on undistributed as well as distributed income. But this would not collect in full from large stockholders who owe the revenue system a tax on their accruals at surtax rates. These could be reached later by a capital-gains tax (departing here from the British) stripped of its present privileges and loopholes.[3]

Concluding this section, we may observe that except as it applies to undistributed profits, the corporate tax is not rationally defensible and should be deemphasized when revenues permit and when even more irrational features have been eliminated.[4] The plausible case for the corporate tax is that we employ other taxes that have even less claim to rationality and that aggravate inequalities in addition.

Averaging

The kind of income tax we need for the postwar period is one that gives maximum feasible concessions to irregular in-

[2] See the author's *Postwar Taxation and Economic Progress*, McGraw-Hill, 1946, p. 219.

[3] See *Postwar Taxation and Economic Progress, op. cit.*

[4] The author is aware of reports that the current profits of corporations after present taxes are "staggering." While no investigation of the reports has been made, it seems probable that present corporate earnings are excessive. The premature repeal of the excess profits tax (before effects of the war had been largely eliminated) is partly responsible. At all events, the priorities here presented preclude important corporate tax changes until conditions are normal. The priorities include the proposition that no reductions should be contemplated until a substantial budgetary surplus has been achieved.

come. Income flows across both time and space, and the necessity of chopping it up according to arbitrary periods and jurisdictions causes no end of trouble. Some attention will be given to jurisdictional matters in the next essay. Here some aspects of the problem of timing deserve consideration.

This matter of timing can produce some weird effects in the income tax. A corporate levy that seems to carry a flat rate may in effect (where there is no carry-forward or carry-back of losses) vary all the way from the nominal rate to one well over 100 percent. A business that earns a million dollars one year and loses as much the next, has a zero net income over the biennium; yet it may pay a very substantial net income tax. An individual who alternates between a $10,000 income and nothing may pay half again as much over the years as one who receives $5000 per annum regularly.

It can be argued, of course, that business and investment losses play a useful role in the economy by directing attention to business mistakes and by eliminating the unfit from business leadership. They may also play a useful role in disposing of surplus capital. Indeed, certain critics have argued that had savings not been wiped out by regular and sometimes extraordinary purges we would long since have been surfeited with them. But this is not to argue that the income tax should ignore real differences among taxpayers, counting only their good "breaks" and overlooking their bad ones, at least if the two occur in different years.

If there are any beneficial effects of the failure to offset negatives against positives in the calculation of the income tax over time, the author does not know of them. In the business field, ignoring net losses gives an advantage to large firms whose size enables them to hedge one operation against another in a single year. A single-line firm cannot do this. The incidence of losses, of course, is correlated with the risk assumed by the business. After double-taxing the risk-taker's positive income and (sometimes) ignoring his negative income, we have begun to question the tax system on the score that it might be prejudicial to the maintenance of a dynamic economy! In our present order we are dependent upon the risktaker to engender income, jobs, and taxes. Often enough he "gets away with murder," to be sure, but the tax system in some respects seems to have been singularly unconcerned about him.

The British have the time-honored practice of disregarding casual income and rating a taxpayer for income tax purposes according to his *regular* receipts. This seems to be one of those anomalous institutions with which British life abounds—about as plausible as the British House of Lords. Imagine trying to determine a regular income for Joe Louis, the heavyweight champion! And does anyone suppose that income is any the less potent merely because it happens to come in one splash rather than a regular flow? The problem is to treat it like other income; letting it escape the tax system entirely is no solution. British contributions to good tax practice are many, but surely this is not one of them.

The inequities that result from arbitrary timing of income are readily conceded by fair-minded critics, but what should be done about them is another matter. Generous carry-overs for business losses are not excessively difficult to manage and are likely to be accepted as a feature of our postwar tax system. But averaging of personal income to take account of irregularity is far more difficult. It has been suggested that averaging might take the form of permitting the taxpayer to sum his taxes over a period of years, calculate what his tax would have been were his income distributed equally among the years, determine the difference between the two, and claim the difference as a refund or tax credit. This sounds simple, but it bristles with problems.

To begin with, it involves an enormous amount of recalculation, at least if applied to forty or fifty million taxpayers. Changes in the rate scale or other provisions of law during the period would involve the application of several sets of tax rules. Averaging would be simplest were the government to choose an income tax system, including a scale of rates and exemptions, and abide by it during a long span of years. However, there is also a current interest in flexibility, which looks toward frequent changes of rates and exemptions, perhaps, even in the course of a single year. The taxpayer, too, may have shifted from a joint (family) to a separate (individual) return or the reverse during the period, and this would involve additional complications. Most important of all, probably, would be the necessity of acquiring information concerning income for the years when the taxpayer's earnings were too small to require a regular return.

Questions would also arise as to when, during the taxpayer's life cycle, eligibility for averaging should begin and when it should cease. Should the taxpayer be allowed to carry forward his unused personal exemption for years prior to the time when he first earned a taxable income? For example, should a person graduating from college be permitted to average with his first years of post-college income, the zero or trifling earnings of his college years?

Should averaging be compulsory or optional with the taxpayer, and, if the latter, should it include a choice of the years to be averaged? The answer must take account of the fact that from a succession of years showing substantial fluctuations, considerable difference in the resulting tax will occur, depending upon when the series averaged start and end.

If fluctuations in income were the only variable in averaging, cases would not arise where the new procedure favored the government rather than the taxpayer. But where an additional variable is introduced by a change in rate schedule, claims for additional tax might be mixed with those for refunds. Of course, the taxpayer would not employ an option in the government's favor, but should the law allow the use of this device as a one-way proposition?

Finally, the question may be asked whether the public does not wish to penalize incomes that respond readily to an improvement and decline in economic conditions. During the war there were those who advocated a special tax on the *increase* in personal incomes. Of course, the principle was applied to business incomes, to some extent, through the excess profits tax. If "A" earns a steady income, prewar, war, and postwar, and "B" earns little or nothing before and after the war but has a very high income during the war years, "B" will be penalized less by high war taxes under an averaging system than under an annual accounting system. However, it is debatable whether it is desirable to treat "B" more severely than "A" during the war period. Then, too, an averaging privilege could be suspended during a war.

Certainly there is more to the installation of an averaging system than meets the eye. The author has raised more questions here than he could try to answer even if he knew all the answers. Instead of attempting an answer to the problems here raised, a further question may be put: Does averaging promise so many complications that it is clearly not worth any further investment of effort? This question can be answered and the answer is negative. Even if averaging were confined to the limited number of returns showing substantial capital gains and losses, it would still be worthwhile. Indeed, it is in this area that better timing seems most essential to the achievement of a rational tax system. Within this fairly narrow scope, averaging of some sort should not prove beyond the range of feasibility.

Administration: Evasion and Avoidance

The postwar income tax should be characterized by strong administration. The rationality of this tax could rapidly disappear were its administration weak and were it featured by wholesale evasion.

Of course, we must distinguish between evasion and

avoidance and point out that there are important problems of both in income taxation. Evasion consists of minimizing taxes in violation of law; avoidance, of doing so within legal bounds. An example of evasion is failure to report black-market income or any income known to be taxable. One can be jailed for evasion with intent to defraud. An example of avoidance is to give up smoking and thus no longer pay the tobacco tax. Any tax is escapable if one pays the price of avoiding the conditions on which it is based. Thus one can beat even the poll tax—by committing suicide.

Avoidance of a tax involves no legal culpability and in most cases it is also morally irreproachable. Some Englishmen criticized the patriotism of their countrymen who quit smoking during the war. But probably this was a rationalization to support the critics' own habits of consumption. Some have maintained that sharp practice and excessive zeal in minimizing income taxes should be condemned. Most people, however, accept compliance with the requirements of law as the full measure of a taxpayer's duty.

Of course, even if the taxpayer must be exonerated when he succeeds in avoiding an income tax which reasonable men would agree he should pay, it does not follow that Congress is entitled to a similar clemency. In the opinion of many critics, Congress has left too many loopholes in the income and death tax statutes. Indeed, there is reason to believe that some of this failure to tighten the tax laws is deliberate. There are those in Congress who calculate, cynically, that high rates are a bone to throw to the demagogic masses and that these rates can and should be made ineffective by leaving holes in the tax fences. This is playing reckless politics with the tax laws and throwing concern for equity and rationality out the window. Usually it is very good strategy (except politically) to trade a reduction of rates for the closing of a loophole.

Space does not permit an analysis of the loopholes in our

present income tax laws. Unfortunately, there are only a few that all critics would accept as meriting that description. However, all honest critics would agree that an income tax law must be carefully drawn to prevent unfair avoidance. They would also agree that the significance of loopholes increases geometrically as the income tax advances in rates and importance.

Evasion, of course, presents problems of a quite different order. There are large areas of income, such as wages and salaries, where collection at the source makes evasion impossible. But there are also large areas such as the income of farmers, unincorporated business, and the professions, where reliance must be placed on the taxpayers' integrity and on such administrative techniques as auditing. The integrity of the taxpayer is not an inconsiderable asset. One administrator, known by the author, estimates that ninety percent of the taxpayers are scrupulously honest in tax matters. (The percentage, he agrees, would sink rapidly if the impression got abroad that most people were "chiseling" on their income taxes.) The income tax is a prime example of a tax that could not be applied at all (or at least not over much ground) if moral levels were very low. Its present vogue is an answer, perhaps, to those among us who argue that our people are well along on the road to moral decadence. However, the government can do much more than it is doing to support the moral backbone of the honest taxpayer. The matter is particularly important now that the income tax has been extended to include the residents of the crossroad village. Moreover, the needs of police work run counter to the tradition of enforcement agencies—to look for fugitive revenue only where it is thickest. We have had one experience with a self-enforcing tax—the intangibles property tax—where the weakness of administration resulted in a sad demoralization. No stone should be left unturned to avoid a repetition.

CHAPTER IV
Income Versus Property Taxes for State and Local Governments
Taxation and the Problem of Federalism

OUR American system of government is usually described as a "federal system," by which is meant that a sovereign national government divides the field of governmental powers with its constituent sovereign states. At least in our early history we were heavily committed to the philosophy of federalism. That the federal idea had been a unique American achievement was the cause of much national pride. Speeches were (and still are) dedicated to the necessity of maintaining a nice balance between the centripetal and centrifugal forces in American life. We developed the idea of judicial review to protect the constitution and federalism. Other federal systems have followed our own in many respects but none has given the courts a comparable protective power. This may be taken as an indication of how seriously we took our commitment to federalism.

Nevertheless, there is evidence that our commitment to the federal idea is now by no means as firm as it once was. In many ways technological and economic changes have knit the forty-eight states into a much more closely woven fabric than were the original thirteen. We have a system characterized by much territorial division of labor, interstate trade, and standardization of consumer goods. (If the author were to buy a new hat in Cincinnati, as advised by his family, he could probably buy the same model that he would have chosen in Madison.) Big business has brought important problems which defy the efforts of forty-eight parochial legislatures. For better or worse, and we think mostly the former, federal powers have been expanded by interpretation to cope with this situation. There are some who go so far now as to say that federalism is antiquated; that it should have been regarded as only a stage in the evolution from a loose confederacy to a unitary state and that we are now ready for the final phase of development.

Fortunately, however (in the author's opinion), this is not the predominant view. We have a very large country and, although in some respects our way of life is uniform and we are firmly united, in other respects this is not the case. There is still a vast difference between North Dakota and New York. A labor law or a liquor-control law that would fit one might seem quite inappropriate for the other.

The federal idea is now finding new application in the attempt to germinate world government. Either the United Nations will evolve toward federalism with some delegation of sovereignty to the central body in areas where it can function appropriately or the experiment will not succeed at all.

Moreover, unitary states do not escape the problem of dividing *responsibility* even though ultimate *power* is completely centralized. Great Britain is a unitary state, yet it allows considerable local self-government. British political scientists have expressed a very lively concern about the efficiency and vitality of local government. Our own municipalities fight for "home rule" as a delegation of power even though they have no claim to ultimate authority. They say that best results in government can be anticipated where communities are allowed to make their own decisions on matters that principally concern them. Participation in government is wider and more vital when it is held close at home. Government *by* the people as well as *for* them is an essential of democracy.

Now all of this has an important bearing on finance. An essential element in the exercise of power is the availability of resources to make it effective. The confederacy that preceded our present federal union showed weakness in the central government's lack of independent sources of revenue. There is an old adage that "the man who pays the fiddler calls the tune." Put the mayors and city councils on the state payroll and see what happens to municipal "home rule"!

Thus, those who believe in local self-government and its importance are forced to direct some attention to the financial systems of states and municipalities. Early in our country's history, the pattern of finance was simple, with federal and state taxation quite sharply divided. The federal government relied mainly on the tariff and the states on the property tax. Gradually, however, and particularly in recent years, both levels of government, subject to the pressure for new revenue, have broadened their tax systems. This movement was strengthened by the fact that many critics disliked tariffs and expressed equal disapproval for the property tax. The result has been overlapping taxation in the fields of income, death, excise, business, and motor vehicle taxation.

It is not our purpose here to inquire into the many problems arising from overlapping taxes. Our present concern is the tax systems of the states and how they may be improved. Nor can all the aspects of state and local finance be here considered. What we can try to do is to place ourselves in the position of a municipal mayor (and what applies to him in large part goes for a state legislator) and consider the major alternative tax sources to which he can look for revenue.

Let us first, however, briefly look at the record. Modifications in state and local finance have been occurring for many years; but under the extraordinary pressures of the depression of the thirties, the pace was so accelerated that the changes have frequently been described as revolutionary. Although the property tax continues to be the overwhelmingly important and sometimes the almost sole support of local governments, it is no longer the principal means of state support, and some states have discarded it entirely. Motor vehicle taxes, state income taxes (two-thirds of the states), business taxes (under a great variety of names and formulas), excise taxes (particularly in liquor and tobacco), and general sales taxes (half the states) all scored important gains during the thirties.

Of the states with an income tax, all but one (Wisconsin) took this step after the federal government had entered the field in 1913. The federal government worked the field exhaustively during World War II but, with two exceptions (South Dakota and West Virginia), the states retained their own levies. The experience was different in other federal systems—notably Australia and Canada—where the income tax became a monopoly of central governments. In these countries the states were compensated for revenue lost by surrendering the tax. Our own federal government continued to facilitate the maintenance of state taxes by allowing them as a deduction in calculating the federal base. This policy, in effect, gave the states priority in the field, enabling them to recoup considerably from the financial famine of the thirties.

The experience of the states with the net income tax has been somewhat disappointing on the quantitative side. The picture is influenced by the fact that a third of the states, including some of the wealthiest, have no state income tax at all. In 1940 only three states derived more than twenty percent of their state tax collections (less of state and local) from this source.[1] The state income tax came into its own during the war, but even then, in all but two years, sales taxes (in twenty-four states) continued to bring in more revenue than the more widely used state income tax.[2]

To some extent municipalities have also participated in state income tax revenues. They have done so through reduc-

[1] U.S. Treasury Dept., Committee on Intergovernmental Fiscal Relations, *Federal, State, and Local Government Fiscal Relations*, Senate Document No. 69, 78th Congress, 1st Session (1943), pp. 433-34.

[2] U.S. Census, *State Tax Collections in 1945 (Preliminary)*, Aug. 1945, p. 5.

tion or elimination of state property taxes made possible by revenues from the income tax; through shared taxes and grants; and (in a few cities) through the development of an independent municipal tax.

With this as a background, let us proceed with the problem as it appears to our mayor.[3]

State and local governments are at the fiscal crossroads. On their postwar route of expanding needs, they have four alternative directions in which to go.

The road to the north marked "General Property Tax" is a familiar highway. But it is not a popular choice for many reasons, most of them impregnably valid.

On the theoretical side, most taxes are tested in terms of their relation to the benefits received by the taxpayer or to his ability to pay. On neither count is there much to say for the general property tax. As to benefits, the point is often made that the fire and police departments of local governments involve property-service expenditures. Where would the property owner be without these services? Would he not try to provide them cooperatively were the government out of the picture? One answer is: Where would any local dweller be without these services? A general benefit justifies a tax but there is no clear apportionment of such benefit to indicate what kind of tax. Even if we were to concede that property alone is the beneficiary of these local services, the value of individual property would be an exceedingly rough index of benefits among property owners. A valuable fireproof building might depend less on the fire department than would a valueless "fire trap," and an idle lot might not receive as much protection from the police department as would a less valuable automobile.

The case for the property tax is at even a greater dis-

[3] The remainder of this essay is an adaptation of an article by the author, "Income Versus Property Taxation for State and Local Governments," *Journal of Land and Public Utility Economics*, Madison, Nov. 1946.

advantage in terms of ability to pay. It is a "debtors' tax," allowing the owners of real estate no offset for liabilities. Frequently, to avoid double taxation and difficult administration, it ignores the well-to-do creditor. Universally it ignores "wealth" which takes the form of personality (not to be confused with personalty) ; education, skill, talent, experience, and the like, may possess first-rate exchange value but they are immune to the property tax.

Then too, the property tax, though nominally proportional, is actually regressive on two counts. For a variety of reasons, assessors usually assess property of low value at a higher ratio (of assessed to true value), than they do property of high value. The most innocent of these reasons is that the high-valued property is less familiar to the assessor and that, when he must indulge in guessing, he does so conservatively. In the second place, the property tax is regressive because it is a levy on shelter for which the poor pay a greater percentage of their incomes than do the rich.

Speaking of shelter, one may recall that at the time of Adam Smith a prevailing practice was to tax individuals on the number of doors and windows in their houses. This was criticized as a penalty on desirable light and ventilation. Now we ignore these particular features of a house, but we do tax the whole house and with much the same effect. At a time when inadequate housing is the topic of the hour and when subsidies for low-cost housing are extensive in practice and legion in proposal, a local tax system that penalizes housing is, to say the least, suspect.

It is generally recognized, of course, that the property tax is as amenable to criticism on its administrative as on its conceptual side. The way to better administration, however, is open and clear enough. Some centralization and professionalization of the assessment position plus first-class state supervision and equalization could do the job, at least if intangible property were excluded from the tax base. We can have better property tax administration if we go after it; but even were we to achieve this objective we might not have a satisfactory basis of local taxation.

Nevertheless, there are some points in favor of the general property tax. It does suit local need for an independent revenue source. Then too, insofar as it taxes land values, it accords with an ancient and valid doctrine that land is a suitable object of taxation.[4] Few sensible people have any illusions that property taxation could be abandoned entirely. There are many, however, who feel that the property tax is already overworked and they are especially skeptical about expanding it further.

Let us, then, inspect the other roads extending from our intersection. The one to the south is labeled "Sales Tax." Its reputation is even worse than that of the northbound highway.

Some people contend that a tax on the "breakfast table" is no more regressive than one on shelter.[5] But they are almost surely wrong. It may be that miscellaneous commodities (taxed by the sales tax) have the same relative importance as does shelter in the budget of rich and poor. However, the property tax often falls on landlords and, according to the standard theory of incidence, is passed along to tenants only partially. Particularly that part of the property tax based on land values is often capitalized and, by reducing the value of land, constitutes a burden on past and present landowners rather than on land-users.

It would seem that if the reformers of local taxation offer only the substitution of one regressive tax for another, we had better let sleeping dogs lie. Or we might conclude with the classic remark of Professor Seligman that "the sales tax constitutes the last resort of countries which find themselves

---

[4] Further discussed in the next chapter.

[5] A tax is said to be regressive when it takes a higher proportion of small than of large incomes.

in such fiscal difficulties that they must subordinate all other principles of taxation to that of adequacy."[6] This conclusion still commands the loyal support of most students of taxation despite the fact that a general sales tax was inaugurated by a labor government in Australia and by liberal Mayor La-Guardia in New York City. Recent innovations and proposals in New York City leave one wondering when that supposedly enlightened metropolis will revive the medieval salt tax!

It can be said that the sales tax makes up to some extent in the opportunistic virtues for what it lacks in rationality and equity. At least it robs nobody very much at any one time. If some intelligent and humane highwayman were to place himself at the entrance to your campus and exact a penny from all who enter or depart, he could gather a lot of booty in a year and no one would feel much the poorer. This exemplifies a principle of operation well known to tax men for many years.

Then too, the sales tax gathers a few "shekels" from those who are passing through. Again referring to the possibility of my purchasing a hat in Cincinnati, I reflect that should I do so, I might leave perhaps thirty cents as a token contribution to the public finances of Ohio. But then again I may decide that the old hat will do for a few more days.

One can say for the sales tax, without departing from Professor Seligman's conclusion, that it may be desirable when other alternatives, for one reason or another, are not available. That is, it may be preferable to starving the public services.

Let us then look to the west. Here we find a road marked "State and Federal Aid." If the municipalities must spend more money, let them ask the central governments for funds. These central units can raise the wherewithal for aid programs from defensible taxes such as the income and estate taxes—at least the federal government can.

[6] E. R. A. Seligman, *Studies in Public Finance*, Macmillan, New York, 1925, p. 131.

However, this road is not all downhill and smooth pavement either. That the aids are a useful device, especially for ensuring a minimum of public services in underprivileged areas, might be generally conceded. When they go further, involving the collection of revenue in wealthy urban centers and the circuitous routing of this revenue to the treasury of some central government and back again, they are not so readily acceptable. The circuitous routing means a loss of proprietary interest in the funds and a sacrifice of local independence. Would it not be better were New York City to rely on its own resources instead of sending a lobbyist, hat in hand, to Washington, particularly with Washington itself collecting so heavily from New York City?

As to the matter of independence, one recalls the prophetic comment of President Jackson that "money is power, and in that Government which pays all the public officers of the States will all political power be substantially concentrated."[7]

It may be that the road most municipalities are seeking is one offering a new *independent* source of revenue. If so, the advice to take the road west will have a most unsavory flavor. Again, this looks like only a last-resort alternative.

There is still the road east bearing the sign "Income Tax." Over half the states have accepted this outlet for part, though usually a minor part, of their traffic. Recently even a few municipalities, notably Philadelphia, Toledo, and St. Louis, have ventured on this broad highway.[8] They have launched forth, however, over the protest of many tax critics who believe this road should be closed to all but the heavy trucks of the federal government.[9]

[7] *Messages and Papers of the Presidents, 1789-1902*, edited by James E. Richardson, Washington, D.C., 1933, III, 67.

[8] Edward Roesken, "Municipal Income, Sales and Use Taxes," *Taxes*, Vol. 24. No. 10, Oct. 1946, pp. 972-78.

[9] For instance, see James A. Maxwell, *The Fiscal Impact of Federalism in the United States*, Harvard Economic Studies 79, Harvard University Press, Cambridge, Mass., 1946.

Several grounds are cited for barring state and local governments from the use of an independent income tax. One is that income is national in character and that it cannot be divided for purposes of taxation by states and subdivisions. Some income is earned in one state and received in another and some corporate income is earned by business which crosses many state boundary lines. The states have employed a variety and diversity of bases and formulas in the allocation of income with the result that some income is taxed twice or more and some escapes taxation entirely. Committees of the National Tax Association have repeatedly studied the diverse practices of the states and have recommended model procedures for the division of interstate income.[10] A few legislatures have taken action along the lines of these recommendations. Others have gone "their own sweet way," with no apparent awareness of any problem. The Supreme Court has mainly side-stepped the confusion. Deduction of state taxes against federal and retention of moderate rates by the states have prevented the problem from growing unbearable. There is little evidence as to the amount of injustice and frustration involved. Unquestionably, much could be done to alleviate the problem were the states awakened to its importance. However, students of interstate fiscal relations have properly recognized this weakness in state levies as a major limiting factor in the further exploitation of the income tax field by the states.

It is also argued, for barring states and municipalities from the income tax field, that the cost of multiple administration and compliance is, or might be, prohibitive. Such evidence as we have[11] of these costs does not indicate that they are in this range, though of course it would be desirable to eliminate

[10] *Proceedings of the National Tax Association* (1938), pp. 486-500; (1941), pp. 583-603.

[11] James W. Martin, "Costs of Tax Administration: Examples of Compliance Expenses," *Bulletin, National Tax Association*, XXIX, No. 7, Apr. 1944, pp. 194-205.

waste wherever possible. This could be done with little or no sacrifice were we to develop a system of central administration and collection of local taxes. Local governments would use the same tax base as do the central governments and simply add on a rate at their own discretion (though perhaps within limits) which the central government would apply and collect for them.

Finally, it is alleged that the federal government is unable to exploit the income tax to the fullest extent while states and municipalities clutter up the field. This argument figured heavily in the decisions of Canada and Australia to nationalize their income taxes during World War II. To be sure, the deductibility of state and local taxes in calculating the federal tax takes some of the edge off this argument. But it is also alleged that only the federal government can apply progressive rates successfully because the smaller units are obliged to tax some incomes in part only. However, this can also be interpreted as good reason why the states, rather than abandon the income tax field, should confine themselves to a broad-based tax with moderate progression. Cities might confine themselves to a strictly proportional tax. Of this, more later.

However, there is a big boulder on the income tax highway which state and local governments are obliged to confront and which the federal government happily can by-pass. This represents cyclical and other fluctuations in tax receipts that attend the imposition of an income tax. Frequently described as a "fair weather" tax, statistics indicate the income tax to be the most "cycle-sensitive" of any major revenue source. In sixteen of the nineteen states that had income taxes during the period 1929-1940, annual yields of this tax fluctuated within the range of 2 to 1 and 8 to 1.[12] This instability is no worse than that of the federal tax, but the

[12] Data were assembled from census reports; *Tax Yields*, Tax Institute, Philadelphia, Pa., 1941; and *Tax Systems*, 6th to 9th editions, Commerce Clearing House, Chicago.

states are in a far less favorable position to take such revenue gyrations. A reduction of fifty percent in the yield of an important state tax is a calamity. The federal government, with its monetary powers and credit elasticity, might consider a fluctuation of this kind an advantage. The tendency of this federal tax to fluctuate in yield has been described as "built-in flexibility," and highly praised.

As for the states, the depression experience of Wisconsin is illuminating. Of course, the public payroll of the state refused to accommodate itself in any great degree to revenue fluctuations. Over a period of twelve years the state subsisted to the extent of about $30 million upon the diversion of tax receipts ostensibly collected for highway purposes.[13]

This took the form of a nominal delay in the authorization to spend these funds according to their intended purpose. No great harm resulted, to be sure, but those interested in highways resented the role in which they found themselves—that of insurers of the state's liquidity. In 1945, over the Governor's veto, the legislature insisted on the future "segregation" of highway funds.[14] Where the state will go for "insurance" in the future remains to be seen.

The experience of Indiana is also enlightening. During the depression a governor had been elected on a platform calling for a net income tax. Once in office, he apparently decided that the net income tax could not be relied upon to lift Indiana out of the financial mire.[15] Accordingly, the administration shifted its support to a gross income tax. The latter may seem to resemble a net income tax, but in its incidence it is probably much more akin to a sales tax. The qualifying "probably" is necessary since the economic effects of a gross income tax are both uncertain and capricious. The

[13] *The Wisconsin Taxpayer*, Wisconsin Taxpayers Alliance, Madison, Dec. 1, 1945.

[14] Laws of 1945 (Wisconsin), Chapters 358, 391.

[15] Franklin P. Hall, *The Indiana Gross Income Tax*, unpublished doctoral dissertation submitted in 1945, University of Wisconsin.

principal defense of the tax is that it applies to a broad base and robs nobody very heavily.

In Wisconsin, municipalities have participated in the income tax through "sharing"; that is, fifty percent of the collections from the normal tax are returned to the cities, towns or villages "of origin." Shared income taxes have been characterized by great diversity in their contributions to local budgets and by ranges in yield surpassing, in most cases, those of state income taxes.

Of the eighteen largest Wisconsin cities, the range in yield between 1929 and 1944 was from 6 to 1 to 77 to 1. The range in average percent of total taxes (income taxes to total taxes over the entire period) was from forty-two percent to seven percent.

A hopeful antidote for instability is the development of reserve funds, as recently recommended by the Moore Committee in New York State.[16] Reserves could be used at either the state or municipal level and could contribute substantially to even the flow of available income tax revenue. Reserves are well worth trying but they confront obvious difficulties: they are subject to diversion following a change in administration and they cannot be planned according to any established pattern of cyclical behavior.

There is also the possibility of developing a new species of income tax along the lines of the experiments now in operation in Philadelphia, Toledo, and St. Louis. These experiments differ among themselves but in general they apply a low flat rate of tax on all net income, with no credits and no deductions except for expenses involved in creating the income. These taxes are collected at the source as far as possible. They apply only to income earned within the municipality and exempt income received from intangibles although the latter is not a necessary feature. A general tax might require some

[16] *New York Times*, Dec. 31, 1945.

state-imposed rules to prevent multiple taxation. This type of levy could be used by states, or municipalities, or both.

An income tax along lines recently developed by these American cities will be criticized as inequitable because it allows no personal credits and carries a flat rate. As to the absence of credits, several rejoinders are possible. One is that the alternatives to the net income tax—the property tax and the sales tax—also offer no exemptions, or at least none designed to allow the taxpayer his family living expenses. This, of course, is defending the tax on the ground that at least it is no worse than are the available alternatives.

The advantage of disallowing exemptions is that the resulting base is large, stable, and conveniently adapted for collection at the source. A halving of community income typically means a reduction of the tax base to a fifth or sixth of its former size. A tax base of the type here contemplated would suffer only the same loss as income itself.

The most convincing reason for exemptions is that they differentiate among taxpayers according to dependents. The differentiation is required to make the tax accord with ability to pay. It would be desirable, if feasible, to allow at least some very limited exemptions in any income tax.

The flat rate of tax is more easily defended. It facilitates collection at the source and avoids reliance upon an unstable element in the income tax revenues. A proportional tax, of course, does not perform the function of equalizing income, but perhaps the equalizing role should be left mainly to the federal government. At the worst, this tax is genuinely and consistently proportional, which is more than can be said for either the sales tax or the property tax.

Two taxes at the state level—perhaps a normal and a surtax—might be the answer. The former would be addressed primarily to the achievement of adequate and relatively steady revenue; the latter to an equalizing role and the maintenance of a progressive element in the tax system. If an additional

[83]

tax is to be applied by municipalities, it should be confined by state law to the larger ones. Duplicate administration and compliance should be avoided by the states serving as agencies for their subdivisions.

It seems in order at this point to digress a bit and recall the debate that preceded the inauguration of the income tax in this country.

Writing in 1911, Professor Seligman in his treatise on the income tax concluded: "Whatever may be the future of the income tax in the United States, it has no prospects as a state tax. In this conclusion almost all serious students agree."[17]

Cited against the state income tax was the evidence of its failure in practice. In addition, it was said that the state is too small a unit in which to apply effective collection devices such as withholding. To collect large amounts from corporations, following the British procedure, nationwide jurisdiction would be required. Seligman stressed the difficulty of dividing income, much of which was national in origin. Other critics emphasized the hazard of state income-tax pioneering; wealth and income would flee from such territory to an untaxed community. If both the states and the federal government were to enter the field, embarrassing double taxation would result. Thus it was concluded that the state income tax would be a backward rather than a forward step. Opponents of this view (very few in number) had "not taken a sufficiently long look ahead."[18]

Professor T. S. Adams was one of those opponents. At the 1910 American Economic Association meeting, in a paper entitled "The Place of the Income Tax in the Reform of State Taxation,"[19] he conceded the weight of expert opinion against

---

[17] E. R. A. Seligman, *The Income Tax*, Macmillan, New York, 1911, p. 425.

[18] Papers and Discussions of the 23rd Annual Meeting of the American Economic Association, 1910, p. 334.

[19] *Ibid.*, pp. 302-21.

state income taxation but asked for a rehearing on the issue. He rebutted the evidence as to failure in practice with the proposition: "We have merely played at state income taxation in this country; we have never given it a fair trial."[20] He went on to cite the substantial success of several European experiments, particularly those of certain German states. These territories had areas and populations comparable to those of our states and they did not rely on collection at the source. As to duplication with a possible federal tax, no great difficulty would result were state rates kept moderate. The same answer could be made to those who feared migration to escape the tax. He admitted difficulty in allocating income to state boundaries, but thought a tolerably equitable system could be devised.

Taking the offensive, Adams cited the conspicuous failure of one element in existing state sources of revenue—namely, the personal property tax. He regarded this failure as inevitable largely because property would not lend itself to lump-sum assessment but required appraisal by items. On the other hand, an over-all assessment of income could be based on "external indicia," such as the taxpayer's dwelling and his general mode of life. Adams then went on to consider alternative reforms. The single tax on land would run counter to the view that land was already overtaxed. The classified property tax was regarded as more promising but it confronted imposing difficulties of administration. The income tax struck a responsive chord in the hearts of the voters. What, he concluded, do the experts have to offer the people of Wisconsin?[21]

Conclusion

This essay has suggested that states and municipalities are at the fiscal crossroads and that none of the available routes to new revenue are clear of obstacles. Some will argue that the obvious answer is that municipalities are spending quite

[20] *Ibid.*, p. 306.   [21] *Ibid.*, p. 321.

enough and probably too much as it is. Of course, economy in the expenditure of public money is always important. But also true is the fact that the local public should be able to express its preference between public and private expenditure of its own income. If the choice be to devote a large proportion of the new fruits of economic progress to public schools and parks, it should not be frustrated by antiquated tax machinery. Thus we cannot avoid in some cases facing the alternatives posed above. The reader will have surmised that the author wishes to focus favorable attention upon the fourth of these alternatives—the use of the income tax for state and local revenue. He is disinclined to accept the view that the successful use of this tax for state and local purposes is beyond the ingenuity of statesmanship and that the state and local tax systems must be confined to regressive and otherwise distasteful levies. He is biased in favor of virile local self-government and a sound financial system to sustain it. The hope of the future in municipal finance lies in the integration of property and income taxation. This involves the mobilization of the vast resource represented by income-earning "assets" other than tangible property. Our municipal finance institutions have failed to keep pace with the changing character of cities, with their centrifugal growth and development of "service" income. If the essay arouses some interest in or support for this point of view, it will have accomplished its purpose.

CHAPTER V

Unity Versus Diversification in Taxation
Neutrality in Taxation

A POSSIBLE canon of taxation is, as suggested in our first essay, that taxes should be neutral among taxpayers. A completely neutral tax might be defined as one that in no way disturbs the allocation of resources which would occur without the tax. A moment's reflection will bring the realization that there is not now and never has been such a tax. To ask for a completely neutral tax in this sense is to ask for one that has no economic effects, and the author knows of no such tax.

The distinction between taxes and fines lies mainly in differences of intent. The former are levied presumably with major intent to raise revenue; the latter to punish for violation of police regulations. But the motivation of a tax may be mixed and its *major* intent difficult to discern. Moreover, quite regardless of the major intent, a tax may have important economic effects aside from its revenue yield.

The term "neutrality" might also be defined as impartiality of treatment. This would call for reasonable classification and a rational basis for tax levies. Discrimination would rest upon a public purpose and avoid arbitrary and capricious distinctions.

If legislative bodies sometimes seek to confer favors and administer punishment through the tax system, they may also seek to maintain neutrality in all senses of the word. Thus it seems probable that Congress would prefer a tax system which is neutral among the several competing forms of transportation—railroads, airlines, trucking companies, bus lines and the like. Large sums of money and much perspiration have been devoted to determine how this end might be achieved, but the answers are still in the area of disagreement.

We may conclude that taxation cannot avoid economic effects and cannot treat all alike. The best to be hoped for is intelligent and judicial classification based on a public purpose. Taxation is an art of selection and of impartial discrimination. This essay considers some possible grounds of classification—of selecting taxes to the best advantage.

Tax Differentiation: On Moral Grounds

Selection or classification may be based on a number of grounds, one of which is ethical. Legitimate or morally superior income or wealth, or the use of such income or wealth, might be given preference over that which is illegitimate or morally inferior.

Let us first consider the possibility of differentiating income for income tax purposes according to a moral classification. Of course, the graduated personal net income tax ordinarily involves quantitative classification only. Even this levy is far from neutral in its economic effects, but it is more nearly neutral than one that differentiates on qualitative grounds.

Differentiating income for income tax purposes on moral grounds confronts important difficulties. Obviously, income differs in moral quality ranging all the way from the fruits of honest toil, approved by everyone, to the profits of illegal activities such as thievery, bootlegging, and black markets, scarcely sanctioned by anyone. We might try to penalize income from an illegal source but it would probably be no easier to find and tax such income even at general rates than to prevent the illegal activity by rigid law enforcement in the first place. It is common knowledge that most income from black-market operations has generally not been reported on income tax returns. This represents a rich field for postwar auditing. Both the purchase of black-market goods for resale and the operations necessary to keep the procedure secret involve extraordinary expenses which are not deductible and can be penalized. In general, the income tax law is content to tax illegitimate income at the usual rates—if indeed the administration can catch up with it all.

However, much income is neither black nor white but rather some intermediate shade of gray. Thus there is a question about the moral standing of income from speculation and risk-taking. Speculative gains are always on the defensive and there are many critics who refer to the stock and commodity exchanges as "casinos." It is true, capital gains are given a privileged position in the present income tax laws but the privileges do not extend to short-term gains, sometimes designated as speculative. The favors to long-term gains can be supported on grounds other than moral ones. That business profits are viewed as immoral by some can be implied from the question frequently raised in religious circles: Is the profit motive Christian? To be sure, there are those who make a hero (not to say a martyr) of the risk-taker and picture him as shouldering the necessary risks for an unappreciative public. But others persist in skepticism. As previously indicated, a good case can be made for the view that profits are discriminated against through the combination of corporate and personal taxes. However, they are also favored when they take the form of undistributed earnings. Whether existing practices are based to any extent upon moralistic grounds would be hard to say.

As has been suggested, selection and classification for tax purposes may be applied to consumption as well as income, and it is much more prominent in the former case. For instance, the British impose a higher rate of tax on whiskey than on ale and no tax at all on milk. They give their tax system credit for a considerable improvement in the drinking habits of the English people. A similar interest has no doubt motivated our federal and state taxes on liquor, though fear of encouraging the bootlegger has limited the program. Any attempt to reduce taxes on hard liquor would meet the ob-

jection that cheap whiskey would be undesirable, especially
in this day of high-speed mechanical transportation. Indeed,
the incidence of the whiskey tax is too capricious to be defended on other than sumptuary and opportunistic grounds.

An eighteenth-century writer defended liquor taxes as follows: "If, of two men with the same annual income, one
spends it all in drink and other vices and the other uses it to
improve a piece of land, should not the former pay more to
support government than the other?"[1] The argument here is
half ethical and half economic. It is not extended to cover all
luxuries but only all vices. As far as the argument is economic, its claim to validity is weakened by the advance toward
an economy of abundance in which saving no longer needs to
be encouraged. As far as the argument is ethical, its claim to
validity depends largely on the elasticity of demand for vices.
Where the latter can be discouraged by taxation, a case for the
tax exists; where they cannot be discouraged, taxing them
only results in a bad distribution of the tax load. Of course,
society may wish to punish by fine those who consume goods
not fully approved even though such punishment will have
no effect as a deterrent. But retribution for its own sake has
a low standing among criminologists and is regarded by most
of them as a survival from less enlightened eras.

The decision to tolerate a vice, except for a tax upon its
consumption, represents a compromise that may not rest
easily on the conscience of a Puritan. The realist's position is
that this toleration is not tantamount to approval; if people
will drink and gamble, they will drink and gamble; given
these circumstances, the state may as well divert some fool's
money to constructive purposes. The Puritan will answer
that even this much toleration is tantamount to connivance.
It allows free play for the devil and profits therefrom.

The ultimate in realism, of course, is where the government

[1] See Joseph Dorfman, *The Economic Mind in American Civilization*,
The Viking Press, New York, 1946, Book 1, p. 131.

[90]

goes into the vice business in order to secure for itself all the income from such traffic. Especially conspicuous is the case of the public lottery. This is regarded by some as the perfect substitute for taxes, providing abundant revenue with no pain whatever to taxpayers. But its recurrent proposal is greeted with persistent and valid opposition from the moralists. They say it holds out to people the hope of improving their position by simply waiting for a stroke of luck, thus undermining their will to achieve economic success by the more arduous processes of hard work and thrift.

As one moves from liquor taxes to other so-called luxury taxes, less can be said on sumptuary grounds for the levies. These measures must then be defended for their opportunistic virtues—convenience of payment, ease of collection, and the like. The tobacco tax will serve as an example. The tobacco factory or retail store is a governmental "revenue office" the world over. In this country it is not uncommon to find the tax equal to half of the price paid by the consumer. Time was, of course, when tobacco was regarded as a form of consumption morally inferior to others, but the supposed injurious effects of tobacco on health have not been entirely substantiated by medical research. In most respects tobacco is in a class with other luxuries, using this term to include all outlays not essential to the maintenance of health and civic responsibility. The inelastic demand for tobacco may even mean that a levy on it comes out of the poor family's allowance for essential commodities. (Of course it is not true that the use of tobacco taxes for education diverts money to schools that would otherwise be used for nicotine.) Undoubtedly the fiscal virtues of tobacco taxes are their main attraction. Here is a means of collecting billions of dollars with minimum expense to the government and minimum resistance by the taxpayer. The soundest defense for these levies is that there are worse ways of raising revenue.

Thus, in the application of sumptuary taxes to vices, a

worthy purpose can be achieved only in the case of an elastic demand. Luxury taxes cannot be justified at all except on the ground that some of them bring in considerable revenue with minimum cost and resistance. It is true that excise taxes are optional in the sense that one can avoid them by changing his consumption pattern. One can also avoid property and income taxes by becoming a ne'er-do-well. The difference, if any, is in the degree of pain involved in exercising the option. Inelastic demand suggests considerable sacrifice. Of course, it is comforting to reflect that exercising the option will cause no serious national consequences. But why pick on consumption, as such, at all? An inelastic demand is a positive asset in accomplishing a purely fiscal purpose; thus taxes on tobacco are preferred to those on soft drinks. But probably neither could find a place in a strictly rational revenue system.

DIFFERENTIATION ON ECONOMIC GROUNDS

Differentiation in taxation may also be defended on economic grounds. This is a matter of taxing economic activities and functions in a way that does not destroy necessary incentives. In other words, it is a matter of selecting sources where the supply is inelastic. Here the leading analysis is that of John A. Hobson,[2] who divides income into "economic surplus" and "economic costs." An economic cost represents a payment that must be made on penalty of losing a supply of the productive factors and of the goods they create. An economic surplus is a payment not required to maintain supply. These distinctions have naught to do with morals nor are they concerned with equity—they are a matter of economic strategy. Not only is it good sense to lay taxes where they do not repress needed production; if the required incentives are foolishly ignored, economic forces will adjust themselves so

[2] John A. Hobson, *Taxation in the New State*, Harcourt, Brace, New York, 1920.

that the factors will command higher prices and eventually the tax will come out of surplus as it should have originally. Thus it is not possible to tax costs even if we so wished.

The difficulty in taxing surpluses (excess rewards) and sparing costs (necessary rewards) is that the two are distinguishable (certainly to a legislator) in only a few cases. It seems apparent that a wage income necessary to keep body and soul together is an economic cost. Probably some reward for risk-taking is properly labeled "necessary" profits; enterprise would not be forthcoming without it. The economic rent of land would seem to be largely surplus. The supply of land (as sites) is very inelastic; in some sense it is true that the Creator made the land and little if any can be added to His handiwork. Probably inheritances are mostly surplus. They are windfalls in most cases to the heirs and are probably not too important as incentives to influence the donor's activity during his last years. Beyond this, we know little enough of incentives and elasticity of supply; it is quite probable that there is a substantial amount of surplus in all income.

A word more about "windfalls." By definition they constitute income for which no equivalent has been rendered. It would go too far to say that society disapproves of "luck money" on moral grounds. But such income is properly regarded as especially appropriate for taxation because no incentive need be offered to secure a future supply. Unfortunately, not often can this type of income be isolated.

If income from land and bequests is to be singled out for taxation on the ground that it is largely surplus, the differentiation need not occur within the income tax itself. Land values can be taxed directly and, of course, we have had long experience with the special taxation of death transfers.[3]

[3] One further point concerning cost taxes needs mention before taking leave of the subject. A tax on a cost which procures for the taxpayer a necessity of life need not be shifted nor need it dry up its source. "A" procures only a subsistence income, which includes a certain allowance for shelter; now if the government assumes the responsibility of providing

DIFFERENTIATION ON EQUITABLE GROUNDS

A final type of distinction among prospective tax bases is that some are more able to pay than others. Thus in many income tax statutes, property incomes are given a more severe rate schedule than service (usually called "earned") incomes. Property income is secure against hazards to which the flesh is heir—sickness, accident, and old age. Moreover, property is a second line of defense, so to speak; the recipient could, as a last resort, work for a living. The distinction has much support and probably some validity. But again it is not easily implemented in practice. Does an infirm old lady who receives $1000 per year as an annuity really have more ability to pay than an able-bodied person who receives the same income from services? Of course, it is true that property remains after the owner dies, but this fact can be taken into account with a death tax. At present, the case for the annuitant is strengthened by the fact that the government has already "doctored" the interest rate to her disfavor. Then too, if property income lasts longer than earned income, so also is the tax applied longer. Earned-income credits are complicated and difficult to apply, and the author is not convinced that they add greatly to the equity of a system which already features a graduated income and death tax.

Unity Versus Diversification in Taxation

Some tax students have searched for a single tax which might constitute the entire tax system. Others have argued that any single tax would be a case of putting all the eggs in one basket; that the ideal tax system must be a highly diversified one. The author would accept a middle ground somewhat closer to the former view than the latter. His ideal tax system would need five or six elements but would not seek diversity

"A" with shelter, even though it may at the same time impose a tax upon him, "A's" ability and incentive to continue production need not be diminished.

for its own sake. He holds that there are about this number of strategic spots for the levy of taxes and that an effort to exploit these few points effectively is better than an attempt to levy on a multitude of bases.

However, there are many who would carry diversity much further than the above paragraph suggests. They argue that diversity is an end in itself; that each tax has its limitations, its loopholes, its irritations, its administrative shortcomings; that a diverse tax system with many levies would have a better incidence and encounter less political resistance than one with fewer elements. The objective of the diversity proponents would seem to be a levy on every possible aspect of economic life. In their view, even though many of these taxes were irrational and inequitable, the errors would compensate for each other. However, we have no assurance that the errors in many irrational levies would be compensating and not cumulative. Certainly the incidence of such a system would be so complex as to be largely incalculable. A highly diversified tax system would leave the distribution of the tax burden largely to chance. It is doubtful if any rational objective could be thus accomplished. On the other hand, with levies confined to a few strategic spots, there is some opportunity to write into the tax system the all-important canons of equity, nonrepressiveness, and rationality.

If we were to inaugurate a single tax today, we would almost certainly choose the personal net income tax to serve as *the* revenue-raising measure. Something could be said for such a system, certainly, in comparison with the hodgepodge of levies which we now have. (An outline of state and federal revenue systems can be found in *Tax Systems of the World*; it not infrequently takes more than one very large page to list and give a few skeleton details concerning the members of the system; in 1942, Alabama had over 130 occupation taxes alone!) However, important objectives in taxation would be overlooked in any single tax. Then too, such a tax

[95]

would need to be worked so hard to meet modern revenue needs that its imperfections of administration and definition would be magnified in significance. Were we to rely exclusively upon the net income tax, we would miss the motor fuel tax, soundly based as it is upon the theory that users of our elaborate and expensive highway system should contribute toward its maintenance. We would miss the social security taxes, which quite properly aim at a contributory system of social insurance. We would miss the tax on land, a factor which, because of its inelastic supply, constitutes a strategic spot to apply a levy. We would miss the tax on liquors of high alcoholic content, where a levy is needed to help discourage undesirable consumption. And above all we would miss the death tax, a levy that promotes equality of opportunity, recaptures windfalls, and siphons off redundant savings without seriously affecting incentives.

"OLD TAXES ARE GOOD TAXES"

Any attempt to reform the tax system by featuring the taxes selected above confronts a time-honored doctrine that taxes, like cheese and wine, take on quality with age. Businessmen frequently assert that they don't much care what kind of a tax system they are obliged to work under provided "you don't change it all the time." They have a particular "gripe" against the federal income tax on this score, recalling that the law has been substantially overhauled every few years since its origin. Adjustments to changes are not only economic but psychological. Income taxes at present levels would have been thought quite impossible before we became accustomed to them. Thus in taxation, as in ill health and disappointment in love, "time is the herb that cures all diseases."

The argument here is analogous to that often advanced by lawyers urging judges to observe the sanctity of precedent in common law. The judiciary, to be sure, does reverse time-honored precedents, but it is restrained in doing so by the thought that people rely on stability of the law and would feel insecure were each judge to make new laws according to the capricious circumstance of his individual temperament.

Of course, this is all very conservative doctrine. Were it heeded in all departments of life without qualification, we should never make any progress. "But for the rebel in his breast, had man remained a brute." Perhaps there should be a presumption against change unless a clear and substantial case can be made for it. Anyone with as much itch to make the world over as the present author cannot be expected to go beyond this.

OPPORTUNISM IN TAXATION

The author's preferred taxes also pay scant respect to the so-called practical canons of taxation, such as ease of administration, sufficiency of revenue, and minimum of taxpayers' resistance. We might justify this on the ground that these opportunistic considerations have the weight of political advantage on their side and that this requires a compensatory bias on the critic's part. Yet it should be added that some taxes for the present can be defended exclusively on their fiscal merits. In spite of impressions to the contrary, taxes are difficult to "sell." The evil of the bad ones must be weighted against the good that might flow from more public services. Public expenditures often do yeoman service in raising cultural standards, improving distribution, and promoting production. Frequently these are much underrated by the voter. This is only to concede, however, that a bad tax, as a last resort, may, under certain circumstances, be better than none.

INCENTIVE TAXATION

The selection of taxes, here deemed strategic, offers little scope for what is sometimes called "incentive taxation," meaning by that term the use of special burdens and immunities to discourage one economic activity and encourage another. As the author has stated elsewhere,[4] he hasn't much confidence in such proposals. They too frequently attack the symptoms rather than the causes of maladjustments. One of the best of these ideas is to tax idle money. But, like lowering the rate of interest, this might prove less stimulating than expected. Failure to loan might be due to failure of demand rather than timidity in the supply. Moreover, a tax on hoarding might force money into safe investments (thus bidding up their price) and do little to encourage new enterprise.

However, this is not to say that the conservation of incentives is not a real concern of the tax system. The Hobsonian approach, considered favorably above, is based upon the idea of preserving necessary rewards for services. Unless we are to take the extreme view that a mixed economy has served its day, and that taxation should be devised to hasten its passing, we cannot avoid concern about incentives. Taxation is like dairy farming, not meat production; good husbandry builds up the herd. Taxation does milk the cows of private enterprise but it should draw the line at killing off the animals.

Multiple Taxation

Somewhat related to the problem of diversity in the tax system is the problem of multiple taxation. It would seem that if all revenue were collected by one layer of government through one single tax, the possibilities of multiple taxation would be negligible. However, it cannot be assumed without analysis that multiple taxation is always bad.

In considering multiple taxation, it is necessary first, of course, to distinguish the different species, of which there are at least four.

Species "A" involves multiple taxation of some objects in

[4] See Harold M. Groves, *Postwar Taxation and Economic Progress*, McGraw-Hill, New York, 1946, Chap. XI.

a uniform class and not others. The general property tax sets out to tax all wealth in the community on an impersonal basis. The national wealth may be measured and counted in either of two ways: one, by adding up the values of all tangible items, and the other, by summing the values of all interests (paper) in the material goods. The general property tax adds *all* the material wealth to *some* of the equitable interests in such wealth. This creates multiple taxation of some objects in a (for our purpose, homogeneous) class and not others. This departure from neutrality is largely unintended but is none the less indefensible. A case somewhat similar occurs in the taxation of corporate profits both to the corporation and to the stockholder. This, too, may be the product of confusion rather than intent; probably few people realize that the profit element in income is the victim of any discrimination. Again, however, the discrimination is not easy to defend.

Species "B" of multiple taxation is commonly called territorial. Smith and Jones are in the same economic circumstances but Smith, as contrasted with Jones, is unfortunate in living near a state boundary line with his residence on one side and his source of income on the other. One state taxes him because he resides within that state and the other because his income is earned within its borders. The Supreme Court rightly refuses to arbitrate these conflicting claims; both states have a legitimate interest in Smith's income. The solution is either an agreement between the states to tax only on a situs or residence basis or somehow to divide the tax. When both states assert their right in full, no one can doubt that Smith has a legitimate complaint against the tax system. Something should be done for Smith, however difficult it may be to reach a practical solution.

Species "C" consists of the imposition of taxes on the same tax base by one or more layers of government. Thus the property tax base frequently serves for school district, town, county, and state taxes. In Toledo, Ohio, one finds both a local and a federal tax on income. Duplication of federal and state levies has developed very rapidly in our day of large-scale spending and extends to income, death, liquor, tobacco, and gasoline taxes, to mention only a few of the more important instances. Singleness of levy (as between federal and state governments) holds for the tariff (federal) and the property tax (state *and* local). In both cases the absence of duplication is based on constitutional limitations. Motor vehicle license taxes are now again exclusively state, though the federal government is not debarred from this field and asserted its right during World War II with its still well-remembered windshield-sticker tax.

There is no conclusive reason why state and federal taxes should not duplicate each other. The imposition of two taxes on incomes and inheritances, one by the states and the other by the federal government, may yield the same result as the use of one tax by one layer of government and the other levy by the other government. Duplication can be criticized, however, on several counts, of which the most persuasive is that dual administration and compliance costs are involved. Although studies attempting to determine these costs are not very conclusive or reliable, they indicate that the amount is substantial but not prohibitive. At any rate, these costs would be worth saving if some means to this end could be found wherein the objectionable features did not outweigh the prospective economies. Unfortunately, no such device is clearly and surely available. The one most often proposed is federal collection, state sharing of revenue, although this proposal confronts the difficult problem of finding a proper basis for distribution. For instance, in the case of income taxes, some states have these levies and others, such as Ohio, have preferred to get their income from other sources. Some states have greater need for income tax revenue than others. Federal sharing would have to be on some uniform mechanical basis that could not be easily adjusted to local differences of need and of opinion. Necessarily it involves a loss of proprietary interest that safeguards the taxpayer against reckless spending. Possibly federal sharing might involve as much waste in distribution of revenue as could be saved in eliminating dual compliance and administration.

There are other ways, however, of reducing or eliminating the unnecessary costs of dual compliance and administration. One of these is known as supplementation. This device, as previously explained, aims to set up a tax base that both states and federal government can levy upon, the former at their discretion though perhaps within prescribed limits, with the central unit making the collection for the state at cost. As suggested previously, this device merits further experimentation. Closely related to it is the development of cooperation in administration, culminating in a single base, a single return, and a single administration of the tax.

Among the possible developments of statecraft in this country, the exploration of more cooperation among governments within different sovereign spheres ranks very high. It is not uncommon to observe more active cooperative relations between the United States and Canada than between Ohio and Indiana, and perhaps also than between the United States and Ohio. The coordination of state and federal revenue systems has been on the agenda of national tax associations for years, and enough has been said and written on the subject to have produced some noteworthy achievement. Thus far the chief gain to be recorded is the (largely unilateral) exchange of income tax information. This has been very valuable to the states but it is hoped that other achievements may soon be forthcoming.

Species "D" of multiple taxation is the one most closely related to diversity in the tax system, previously discussed. It consists of two taxes on closely related aspects of the same object of taxation. For example, a gasoline tax, a motor vehicle license tax, and a personal property tax may be levied on the same car-owner or the same automobile. The purpose of the first two taxes is to gauge one's contribution toward the upkeep of highways both by the possession of a car and by the use of it. The personal property tax requires the possessor of wealth in the form of an automobile to contribute to the general support of government. In this situation there are states that apply only one of these taxes and there are states that apply all three. Reasonable men might differ as to which is most advantageous. For our present purposes, it is the triple tax as such that we are interested in. Obviously, it is not necessarily unjust; it treats all in the same class alike; three measures of a car-owner's responsibilities may or may not be better than one, but this is not to be judged *a priori* and without regard for the weight of the evidence.

When state income taxes are added to property taxes, legislators are often troubled by the multiple-taxation aspects of the situation. The Supreme Court has decided that to tax the income from real estate does not differ materially from taxing the real estate itself. Thus, with the broadening of the tax system to include an income tax, income-earning property is subject to a double tax. Some state laws have taken this into account and have allowed offsets of one sort or another to eliminate or reduce this multiple incidence. But the critics have not approved of the offsets and the latter have not gained in favor with the passage of time. The case is not so clear as that of the motor vehicle levies but probably both are instances of taxing different aspects of the same taxable object.

Perhaps the distinct taxation of inheritances and income might be classed as double taxation of the Species "D" type. There are many ways of viewing the death tax. It can be viewed as a tax on the heirs' receipts. This was the view taken in the abortive federal income tax of 1894, which included inheritances as part of the recipient's income tax base in the year of the receipt. More recently, competent critics have advocated an integration of income and death taxes.

The death tax can also be regarded as a delayed and second levy on the income of the deceased. Insofar as the income tax currently levied is lightened to take account of the fact that the portion saved will again be taxed at death, this view is plausible. The death tax can also be thought of as a tax on wealth, independent entirely of income levies.

That the income tax and the death tax are closely related and overlap each other to some extent cannot be doubted. This justifies taking account of the one in fixing the levels of the other. The fact that the death tax falls with special weight on saving might be an argument against its development were our economic situation one in which saving needed to be conserved. Where we have reason to fear redundant saving, however, the death tax is freed of this inhibition and finds additional support because it is timed strategically to offer a minimum impediment to investment. Integration of the death with the income tax through inclusion of the inheritance in the heir's income tax base would give the tax a capricious incidence, at least without a highly developed system of averaging, and it would ignore entirely the aspects of the death tax relating to the deceased rather than the heir. In this case the death tax is properly regarded as a double tax on the saving of the deceased and also a tax on the unearned income of the heir; such duplicity as this may involve is accepted as desirable.

Certain critics have contended that it is double taxation to tax income saved at the time of its receipt and then again to tax the flow of receipts which stem from this saving when received and consumed by the saver. In a sense, the saving has value only as it anticipates or represents a capitalization of the future flows. Similarly, it is called double taxation to tax both a capital gain and the augmented income of the investment which is responsible for increase in the value of the asset. These subtleties fortunately have never percolated to the consciousness of practical-minded legislators. To them the receipt of disposable income is the index of ability to pay and economic power, and both the income destined to be saved and the realized capital gain afford such economic power.

Conclusion

Without attempting to summarize these essays, the author will conclude with a brief recapitulation of the values he has stressed in this survey. As to taxes, strong preference has been shown for those that are rational, that follow some relevant facts in the relationship of taxpayers to each other and to the government. We have accepted the view that taxes should reduce inequalities substantially and have carried this to the point of saying that if the capitalistic system will not take graduated taxation, we had best look for a hardier system. We have recognized that no tax is exclusively for revenue; that taxes must have economic effects; and that strategic selection must seek to conserve the tax base. Least weight has been given to what we have labeled opportunistic considerations; but even here it has been recognized that a bad tax is sometimes better than none; that a tax may take on virtue from the public services it makes possible.

This weighting may seem idealistic but at least there has been no pandering to tax interests tainted with demagoguery. Generous income tax exemptions, easy terms for capital gains and undistributed profits, and discriminatory levies on distributed corporate earnings, have been viewed with due skepticism. Success in plugging income and death tax loopholes has been deemed more important than high rates. Adequate policing of all the area covered by a mass income tax has been judged essential. Treading on the toes of those who think an income tax no good unless graduated, we have suggested that for states and municipalities the development of a very broad-based tax with a flat rate might be the best available means of preserving the highly important fiscal independence of these units.

Touching certain broader aspects of public finance in several essays, notably the second, we stressed the desirability of a pragmatic attitude toward the future role of government. But a positive program and certain institutional changes were deemed essential within this frame of reference. We accepted the view that taxation and public expenditures are among the best available tools for coping with unemployment, and that a shortage of markets is likely to feature our postwar economy, a fact that should constantly be remembered in tax selection.

Obviously, public finance is a large and complicated field and we could attempt to cover here only a few of its more philosophical aspects. Obviously, too, a philosophy of taxation is highly dependent upon a general philosophy of life. Both should change and grow as the philosopher's experience broadens and deepens.